PRAISE FOR *KIDNAPPED BY THE TALIBAN*

"Dilip Joseph, MD, is a physician and humanitarian, but he's also my friend, and he endured an unimaginably difficult ordeal—being kidnapped at gunpoint in Afghanistan. This gripping book is a page-turner from start to finish; however, what I found most surprising and enduring is what Dilip taught me, and will reveal to you, about the mind of the Taliban terrorists. It will challenge everything you think you know."

—WALT LARIMORE, MD

BESTSELLING AUTHOR, *THE GABON VIRUS* AND *THE INFLUENZA BOMB*

"Dr. Joseph is a friend, a colleague, and a person with whom I share a passion for serving the underserved, especially in Afghanistan. Having worked closely with him, when I heard he had been taken by the Taliban, I was deeply concerned for his health and his life. When I learned of his rescue, I was greatly relieved. His moving, transparent account of his experience is both exciting and revealing, as he shares his true care for his captors and his appreciation for his rescuers as well as his deep remorse for those who lost their lives in this tragic event. I was caught up in the story from the very beginning and couldn't put it down!"

—MITCH DUININCK, MD

PRESIDENT, HOPE PARTNERSHIPS INTERNATIONAL

"I was very pleased to meet Dr. Joseph in Afghanistan, where he impressed me with his heroic willingness to serve others in a dangerous place. When I heard that Dilip had been captured by criminal thugs, I feared the worst, especially after having witnessed multiple tragedies in that dark corner of the world. This book is a riveting account of that harrowing story.

"Dilip tells the tale remarkably well, but for me, his most moving tribute to the men in uniform who served with him is of great personal significance. Dr. Joseph and his comrades got a one-in-a-million opportunity for rebirth through these horrific events, and this book offers readers a similar shot at redemption by confronting the inexpressible value of our own personal liberty. Dilip got to see firsthand what the price of freedom looks like. We all can be better people through hearing what he has to say about it."

—TIM KIRK

COLONEL, U.S. AIR FORCE

"Dr. Dilip Joseph's vivid, authentic storytelling offers a rare view into the physical, psychological, and spiritual experience of Taliban captivity. While the threat of death from the captors' pointed AK-47s and Kalashnikovs was unmistakably real, so was the strange intimacy shared between captives and captors around meals of fresh naan and green tea, the human connections that were possible even under the most hostile circumstances.

"Dr. Dilip's unbreakable personal faith in God, along with the courage and resilience of his beloved teammates and fellow captives, Dr. Rafiq and Farzad, resonate throughout the pages of this book. Their ongoing commitment to serve some of the most destitute people on earth living in rural Afghanistan is a moving testament.

"Finally, the sacrifice made by the SEAL rescue team serves as a sobering reminder of the costliness of freedom and the preciousness of each moment of life."

—FARZANA MARIE
PRESIDENT, CIVIL VISION INTERNATIONAL

"You will be amazed, inspired, and humbled by this remarkable story of one man's journey through terrorism, kidnapping, and threat of death. *Kidnapped by the Taliban* is an amazing story of God showing his love to a world filled with hatred. It's an amazing story of how God provides grace and strength in the most horrific of trials. It's a story of God's faithful provision to Dilip Joseph, a dedicated, compassionate doctor who literally laid down his life for the sake of a people in desperate need of God's love."

—WAYNE PEDERSON
PRESIDENT, REACH BEYOND

"I couldn't put this book down. Dr. Joseph's passion and willingness to go wherever God directed him, even when it was away from his family and into a war zone in Afghanistan, show the heart of a humanitarian. *Kidnapped by the Taliban* is also a tribute to the sacrifice and courage that the men and women of the U.S. military serving in Afghanistan show every day."

—CHRISTOPHER BRAMAN
SERGEANT FIRST CLASS, U.S. ARMY RANGERS (RETIRED), AND RECIPIENT OF
THE PURPLE HEART AND SOLDIER'S MEDAL

KIDNAPPED
BY THE TALIBAN

KIDNAPPED
BY THE TALIBAN

A STORY OF TERROR, HOPE, AND
RESCUE BY SEAL TEAM SIX

BY DILIP JOSEPH, MD
with James Lund

W PUBLISHING GROUP

AN IMPRINT OF THOMAS NELSON

Published in Nashville, Tennessee, by W Publishing Group, an imprint of Thomas Nelson.

Author is represented by the literary agency of Alive Communications, Inc., 7680 Goddard Street, Suite 200, Colorado Springs, CO 80920, www.alivecommunications.com.

Thomas Nelson titles may be purchased in bulk for educational, business, fund-raising, or sales promotional use. For information, please e-mail SpecialMarkets@ ThomasNelson.com.

The events described in this book are true. Some names and a few locations have been changed to maintain military security, protect identities, and increase safety for the people involved.

All photographs courtesy of Dilip Joseph, Morning Star Development, and James Lund.

Scripture quotations are taken from the Holy Bible, New International Version®, NIV®. © 1973, 1978, 1984 by Biblica, Inc.® Used by permission of Zondervan. All rights reserved worldwide.

ISBN 978-0-7180-9303-7 (trade paper)
ISBN 978-0-7180-3156-5 (IE)

Library of Congress Control Number: 2014942499

ISBN 978-0-7180-1128-4

17 18 19 20 21 LSC 6 5 4 3 2 1

To my mother, Rosamma "Jolly" Joseph

When you were alive, you were my anchor. Even in death, your memory propels me to serve God and others to the best of my ability. Thank you for the amazing example of your selfless sacrifice of time, energy, and resources to not only our family but also many around the world. My hope is that people who knew you well will be reminded of you in these pages.

CONTENTS

CONTENTS

KIDNAPPED

PROLOGUE

"ARE YOU GETTING ENOUGH PROTEIN IN YOUR DIET? ARE YOU getting enough carbohydrates?"

The questions in Pashto come from Miriam, a local midwife and employee of the same nonprofit I work for. She's addressing twenty moms and kids jammed into a fifteen-by-twenty-foot office. About half of the visitors sit in metal folding chairs while the others stand. Miriam points with a stick to a board beside her. Tacked to the board are plastic baggies filled with nuts, beans, and rice.

Two and a half weeks ago, I was at home with my wife and four children in Colorado Springs, Colorado. Now I am at a medical clinic in Pul-i-assim, a village in eastern Afghanistan. I am the medical director for Morning Star, a non-governmental organization (NGO) committed to helping this nation's people rebuild their country and their lives. This is my tenth visit to Afghanistan. I'm here to deliver a dose of medical training and hope to people who desperately need both.

What I don't know is that I will soon be the one in desperate need of help and hope.

As Miriam speaks, my gaze is drawn to a mother standing near a corner in the back of the room. Her eyes appear locked on the board as she absorbs each word, though I can't tell for certain because she is covered head to toe in a light-blue burqa, which includes a *chadri*, or veil, to cover her face. She holds an infant no more than two months old in her arms. A toddler stands to the mother's left, one hand gripped tightly to his mother. He's coughing repeatedly. On her other side a three-year-old leans against her and wipes her runny nose on her sleeve.

I wonder about this young mother's life. I guess that she is nineteen and lives in her husband's home in a nearby village. I imagine that in addition to caring for her husband and three young children, she takes care of and does all the housework for her extended family—perhaps a mother-in-law and two brothers-in-law. She breastfeeds her younger children but can't produce enough milk to fully feed them, so her husband is forced to buy low-quality formula during his monthly visit to the closest town, straining an already meager family budget. I have no doubt that this young mother often feels overwhelmed.

She is surely not an educated woman. Most girls in rural Afghanistan are expected to quit school after the second or third grade. Yet I can see that she is highly motivated to care for her family. She leans forward, eager to see the pictures describing good nutrition and hygiene and hear every word of advice.

I smile. This is why I am here. It's hard to describe the sense of fulfillment that wells up in me when I view the clear need in the innocent faces of these young children and the strong desire to improve their health and lives in the attentiveness of their mothers. Medical services in rural Afghanistan are so rare. In moments like these I know my team and I are helping to bridge the gap between what is and what can be. The gap is still wide, but we are making a difference.

I am glad to finally be back among these people. It's been a year and a half since my last visit to this clinic. Six previously scheduled trips to the region were canceled due to threats of violence.

The threat is from the Taliban, the Islamic extremists who use terror and force to impose their strict interpretations of Islamic law. The Taliban ruled Afghanistan from 1996 until December 2001, when they were forced out of power by the U.S.-led invasion that followed the 9/11 attacks on America. Yet the Taliban influence here lives on in an insurgency that claims thousands of lives each year. During the Taliban rule, the villagers in Pul-i-assim fled to Pakistan, returning to their homes only after the regime collapsed.

For people living in rural areas where the Taliban influence is strongest, including where we work, the danger is a shadow that never goes away.

After serving at the clinic all morning, my two native coworkers—Rafiq, a physician and local program director for Morning Star, and Farzad, his assistant—and I enjoy a sumptuous lunch hosted by the local police chief. At two thirty in the afternoon, we drop off the police chief and another local doctor near the medical clinic then begin the four-hour drive back to Kabul.

Now, just a few minutes later, we spot a dozen boys walking the same way we're going on the side of the road. We saw these students in the educational facility next to the medical center this morning. They're on their way home, after spending time in computer or literacy classes. When we offer them a ride, they pile into the open truck bed, smiling and grateful for the lift. We let them off in a village about five miles down the road, wave good-bye, and continue down the winding dirt road.

As we drive, I think ahead to my evening plans: dinner and a meeting with my NGO's country director and his wife in Kabul. We're going to discuss current programs and plans for the future. There is so much yet to do here. Then, in another week, I will be home with my family and getting ready for Christmas.

We are traveling in a white, ten-year-old Toyota Hilux. Rafiq is behind the wheel of the four-door pickup for this first leg. I sit beside him in the front seat while Farzad sits in the back.

When we approach a hairpin right turn about fifty yards ahead, Rafiq slows down. Our road is on a hill that gradually declines. To our left, after a short drop, the mountain rises steeply into sunny blue sky. To our right is an equally steep drop into a canyon below.

A tap on the shoulder is my first hint that something is wrong— Farzad is reaching forward to get Rafiq's attention. *What's going on?*

Rafiq slams on the brakes.

Through the windshield, a hundred feet ahead of us on the right, I see him. Next to an outcropping, where he'd obviously been hiding moments before, stands a man. He is wearing a thick, beige jacket over traditional garb. On his head is a brown wool *pakol*, a hat with a kind of double-pancake appearance. He has a long black beard that covers his neck.

What most gets my attention, however, is the ammunition belt around his waist and the Kalashnikov assault rifle in his hands.

The man raises his Kalashnikov—also known as an AK-47—and fires a single shot into the air.

A surreal feeling washes over me. *No, no,* I think. *Is this staged? This can't be real.*

Two more men, also carrying assault rifles, pop out from behind another hill ahead and run directly toward us.

I'm suddenly aware of my heart pumping into overdrive. *This can't be happening. Oh, man. I can't believe this is how my life is going to end.*

One of the pair of men ahead is shouting orders in Pashto. I don't understand a word. Both Rafiq and Farzad open their doors and get out of the pickup. I follow their lead and do the same. As I open my door, a fourth armed man comes toward us from the rear.

This is clearly a strategic action. Which is it—robbery or kidnapping? I hope the latter. Most roadside robbery victims in these rural areas are quickly killed.

Rafiq, Farzad, and I huddle together next to the left side of the Hilux. All four of our attackers begin yelling at us. Rafiq and Farzad raise their hands in the air, so I do likewise. The man who arrived from behind us begins to take charge. He appears to be the oldest, perhaps twenty-eight. His beard is shorter and better groomed and his outfit a lighter brown compared to the rest.

This leader is angry with us. He raises the butt of his rifle as if to strike me with it. I wince, but the blow does not come.

The leader keeps shouting in Pashto. As Rafiq attempts to answer, the leader flings open the back door of the Hilux and grabs the backpacks Rafiq and I brought. He makes an abrupt search. Rafiq whispers to me, "He wants to know why we're here and what we do."

I say nothing and avoid eye contact with the gunmen. Since I am an ethnic Indian, I can easily pass for an Afghan—at least until I open my mouth and those listening realize I don't speak their language.

I don't want to incite these men further by revealing that I'm an American.

All our attackers are dressed similarly. The man we spotted first looks to be in his midtwenties and is the tallest of the group, nearly six feet. The other two, who appeared ahead of us, look nearly as old but may be much younger—with their dust-caked faces and ruddy complexions, it's difficult to tell. The taller of this pair may still be a teen, but he carries himself like an experienced soldier. This one points his rifle at us and gestures for us to step to the side of the road, away from the pickup.

Now what? I wonder. *What are their intentions? Are they going to shoot us right here on the side of the road?*

Suddenly, coming down the same road we'd traveled moments before, a lone man on a motorbike appears. He stops within five hundred feet of us, assesses the situation, and turns around. Seconds after his arrival, he has disappeared. *Will he report what he's just seen?*

One of the gunmen begins tearing a cloth into long strips. He uses one of these strips to tie a blindfold around my head. The makeshift blindfold isn't 100 percent effective. At the upper left corner I have a tiny opening. Since my hands aren't tied, I'm able to tug it down a fraction, providing me with a little better view of what's happening.

I fear this is the end. My mind is functioning just well enough to offer a silent prayer: *God, save me from this situation!*

Our captors attempt to put blindfolds on Rafiq and Farzad as well, but something doesn't work—maybe the other strips are too short. Though it feels like an eternity, it's probably less than ten minutes later when my blindfold is removed.

Now the same strips of cloth are used to tie our hands behind our backs. We're each pushed into the rear seat of the Hilux. The leader climbs into the driver's seat. The second-oldest joins him in the front passenger seat.

My heart rate drops one notch.

Okay. At least this doesn't appear to be a robbery. We're still alive. They're taking us somewhere, so there's some plan here.

The leader shifts the Hilux into reverse and guns the engine. He turns us around, driving so quickly and carelessly that for a moment I think we will career over the road's edge and tumble down the mountain.

My heartbeat resumes its frantic pace.

In a few minutes we reach the village where we'd dropped off the boys. A few of the inhabitants look up as we drive by. I plead with my eyes, *Please notice that this is a medical truck and there are armed men in the back. Please alert someone!*

In no time we are through the village and back on the deserted road, heading for the village and medical center, where we had spent the morning.

This could be good, I think. *It might all go south when we reach the village and police post, but at least people will know what's happened to us.*

But this glimmer of hope vanishes as quickly as it appears. The leader makes an abrupt turn off the road and into a valley. The terrain is rocky, and our captor is driving fast. I'm afraid he's going to either tip over the Hilux or disable it, leaving us stranded in the middle of nowhere.

As we bump along, I attempt to slide my hands over to Rafiq's, thinking I might be able to untie him without being seen. At the same time, I whisper, "Do you have any idea what these guys are thinking?"

Almost imperceptibly, he shakes his head. "No, I don't," he whispers. "We need to keep quiet."

I can't imagine our situation getting any more frightening, but it does. The two kidnappers in front trade angry comments, which I later learn were along the line of, "We will show these donkeys sitting behind their posh desks and computers what real Islamic life is like." Then the leader tries on a pair of sunglasses he finds in the truck. They apparently don't fit, so he smashes them against the dashboard.

He isn't done venting his rage. While holding the steering wheel with his left hand, he rips the rearview mirror from its base with his right. Then he attacks the overhead visor. His number two in the next seat starts doing the same to his visor. Neither is successful at tearing his visor completely off, so each satisfies himself with destroying its shape.

These guys are out of their minds. They could do anything.

After fifteen minutes of this wild driving in a wide valley, we enter a passage through hill country that cuts off any view of the surrounding landscape. Then we stop and are ordered out of the Hilux.

With a jerk of his rifle, the leader points up the mountain on the left. There is no path. I look higher and see more armed men at the top of a hill about two hundred feet above us.

Apprehension surges up in me like black oil from a well. These aren't ordinary robbers. This is too systematic.

I've been kidnapped by the Taliban.

Two of the men grab our backpacks out of the Hilux; then all of us begin climbing. With my hands tied behind me, it's hard to maintain balance on the steep terrain. I'm sorry to leave the Hilux. It is a last remnant of my work here, of normal life.

As we walk, I hear our captors talking among themselves. My

sense is that they are talking about us. I fear the worst—that when we reach the top, they will shoot us.

God, however this is going to end, please don't let them torture me to death. Let it be one shot and done.

It is amazing how quickly everything we take for granted can be ripped away. In the space of a few minutes, I have lost all control of my life. All I can do is take a step, draw a breath, and hope I will be given the chance for another.

Step.

Breathe.

Hope.

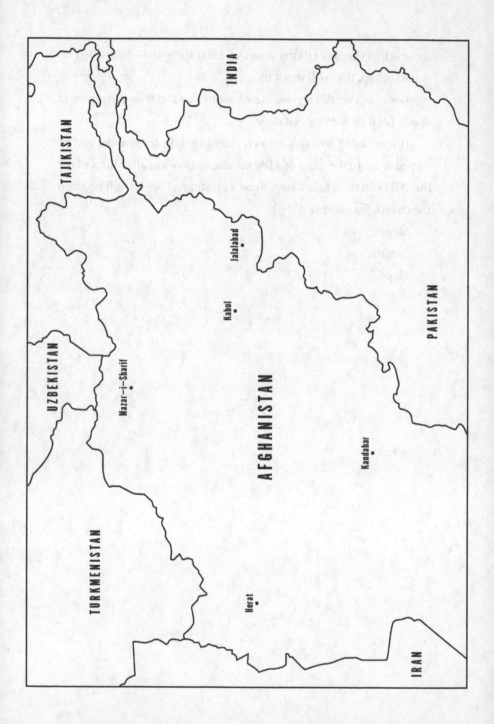

The first time we meet, we are friends. The
next time we meet, we are brothers.

—Afghan proverb

FINDING MY WAY

7:00 P.M., SUNDAY, NOVEMBER 18, 2012
COLORADO SPRINGS, COLORADO
ON THE NIGHT BEFORE MY TRIP TO AFGHANISTAN, THOUGHTS of kidnapping and death were the furthest things from my mind. I was instead relaxing on a couch in my home. My focus was not on the intentions of armed men but on the adventures of a trio of small trucks, otherwise known as *The Three Little Rigs*.

"Little rig, little rig, let me come in!" I read aloud in my best imitation of a talking wrecking ball. "Not by the chrome on my chinny chin chin!" I answered myself, trying now to sound like a young truck.

In my lap sat my son, three-year-old Tobi, his ears absorbing every word and his wide eyes taking in every detail of the picture book I held in my hands. Snuggled next to us was my oldest son, five-year-old Jaron. On another couch across the room, my wife, Cilicia, read a book to our oldest child, eight-year-old Asha. On the floor in a corner, the newest addition to our family, eight-month-old Eshaan, played with his puzzle toy.

I love my roles as husband and father. Anyone with children understands the rewards and joys of raising a family. I had anticipated this

1

before Cilicia and I started having kids. What surprised me, however, was how much my family has taught me—especially about parts of my character that still need work. When money was tight and Cilicia spent more than I thought appropriate on an outing with friends, I realized I was lacking in grace. When my kids were louder before bedtime than I initially thought was necessary, I realized I needed more patience.

Of course, my family also has taught me about each of them. I particularly enjoy uncovering the mystery of each child's personality. Asha, for example, revels in her role as the oldest. She is a born leader, passionate and driven, with a strong sense of justice and fairness. Jaron is more easygoing, sensitive, and reflective. He often comes up with insights that surprise me. Tobiah—we call him Tobi—is what Cilicia terms "a sunshine." He enjoys being the center of attention and knows how to draw others to him through his smiling face, his friendly and persistent questions, and his silly antics.

Eshaan seems to be easygoing, like his brother Jaron, but it is too soon to know much for certain. I especially look forward to understanding him better in the months and years ahead.

Cilicia, meanwhile, is a devoted and incredibly patient mother. She is also an amazingly genuine person with a warm heart. From the beginning of our relationship, I found talking with her encouraging and energizing. After nearly twenty years of these conversations, including a decade of marriage, that still hasn't changed.

I let out a contented sigh as I glanced around the room. Like any married couple, Cilicia and I had our ups and downs. And certainly, raising four young kids isn't always easy. But I realized I am truly blessed. As I approached my forties, I could not imagine wanting any other life.

Yet, once again, I was going to walk away from the people I most cherished and put all this on hold. I tried to freeze in my mind the image of my family all around me. The last night before I traveled overseas always felt bittersweet—my excitement and anticipation over the upcoming trip mixed with the knowledge that it would be a few weeks before I saw my loved ones again.

I would miss them. But this was a call I could not ignore.

You could say that call started with my parents. Both were natives of India, living in Kerala on the country's southwest coast. My father, P. V. Joseph, was in his early twenties and leading a youth group meeting when he met my mom, Rosamma, five years younger. They fell in love. Most families in India, then and now, abide by an arranged marriage system. My father and mother were thrilled when their families connected and sanctioned their union. To commemorate his joy over their new life together, my father began calling my mother Jolly (pronounced Joe-Lee).

My sister, Deepa, was born a year after the wedding. I arrived two years after that, on July 28, 1973.

Kerala is a diverse state, where today more than half the population is Hindu, another quarter is Muslim, and nearly 20 percent is Christian. Both of my parents grew up in Christian households and committed their lives to Jesus Christ at a young age. They launched an independent church movement that included services held in various people's homes. Ours was one of them. People constantly came and went, sometimes staying for days or weeks at a time.

Among my strongest childhood memories, however, is what we did outside of our home. Virtually every weekend we and other members of our home church traveled to another neighborhood to hand out food or help with other practical needs. Even though they didn't have much, my parents made it a priority to do what they could for those who were struggling physically, emotionally, financially, or spiritually.

One of those struggling people was a man my dad came across during one of his monthly hospital visits. Jacob was in his late twenties and desperately needed a blood transfusion. Dad arranged for a businessman in our fellowship group to give blood for the transfusion. At the last minute, however, the donor had to back out. So my dad, even though he has a slight build and is not a particularly strong man, decided to donate the blood himself.

Jacob was so impressed with my dad's efforts that he began attending our home church. Later he even asked my father to officiate at his wedding.

Throughout my childhood my parents demonstrated a great love for each other and for people around them, including those they didn't know. In their way, my parents were rebels, determined to defy the status quo and live out what they believed in. Although I didn't realize it then, their emphasis on love, service, and following one's beliefs made a lasting impression on me.

I was also tremendously impressed by a documentary I watched when I was eleven. It was about a Japanese doctor who traveled to China's remote interior in the late 1800s to offer medical aid and love through his faith. The doctor lived in the villages with the people he served. I realized he had chosen a difficult assignment, yet it was exciting to see the expressions on people's faces—a mixture of caution, curiosity, and appreciation. This courageous doctor was eventually killed by government forces because his presence and beliefs were deemed a threat.

I was inspired by the idea of traveling to another country as a doctor and humanitarian—and by this doctor's commitment, despite the danger. I dreamed of doing the same one day.

When I was fifteen, the traveling part of my dream came true. My dad—thanks in part to the encouragement and prodding of my mom—had moved to the United States two years before to study at Fuller Theological Seminary in Pasadena, California. Once I completed the Indian version of high school, the rest of the family and I joined him.

At first, America overwhelmed me. Everything here was huge. On the drive from Los Angeles International Airport to Pasadena, I was amazed by the skyscrapers, massive bridges, and interlocking concrete freeways.

But I adjusted quickly. I was something of a social butterfly, and when I joined the junior class at Marshall Fundamental High School, I made many friends. I was active, joining the science and key clubs and the tennis team. I enjoyed immersing myself in American culture.

I might have enjoyed myself a little too much. Academic success came easily to me at Marshall, and I didn't challenge or prepare myself as I should have for college. When I enrolled at nearby Azusa Pacific University in 1991, I found the courses far tougher. I didn't make my path any easier when I chose biochemistry as my major.

My time at Azusa was marked by two life-changing events. The first occurred during my junior year when I went to a seminar on polymerase chain reaction, at that time a new biochemical technique. It was chemistry of a different sort, however, that made that class memorable.

The room was packed, fifty people in a space designed to hold thirty. I managed to find a chair in the back row. Right after I sat down, the guest speaker began his opening remarks—except I didn't hear a word. I'd noticed a girl sitting directly in front of me in the next row. I could see only the back of her head and the side of her face, but her long dark hair and attractive features immediately grabbed my attention.

Who is she? Since I didn't recognize her, I decided she must be a freshman.

It turned out that this pretty girl was indeed a freshman, and a family friend of one of my best friends, also a student at Azusa. Cilicia had grown up in both Southern and Northern California. Her father was originally from India while her mother was a Caucasian American who'd also grown up in Northern California.

Cilicia was dating another friend of mine on campus, so I saw her occasionally and gradually got to know her. I enjoyed her company and considered her a cherished friend, but since she was dating someone else, I didn't allow myself to think of anything more.

The next year was my last in college. For my final semester I enrolled in an art history class, one of my last requirements for graduation. I enjoyed the class, but I enjoyed one of my classmates even more: Cilicia. She and her boyfriend had broken up, and the more we talked that semester, the more our friendship grew.

All too soon, however, the course ended. I was graduating and needed to figure out what I would do with my life. Cilicia was thinking about transferring to a school closer to home. After that last art history class, we walked to a McDonald's for a burger and sat down.

"It's been great to get to know you a little bit," Cilicia said with a warm smile.

"It has for me too," I agreed. "I hope you have a fun life. I hope we keep in touch."

We thought we were saying good-bye, but it turned out to be just the beginning. Over the next few months my thoughts kept returning to Cilicia. I missed her friendship and our easy conversations. Something about her was so engaging. We continued to talk occasionally by phone and e-mail, and when she called six months later to let me know she was coming to visit family in the area, we decided to go out for dinner. Seeing her again after all that time, I could no longer hide my feelings from her—or myself. Over pizza in a booth at the Cheesecake Factory in Pasadena, I confessed that I was strongly attracted to her. I was thrilled and relieved when Cilicia said she felt the same way.

Amid all the uncertainty in my life, this felt right. It was the start of a long-distance and very long-term courtship.

The second transforming event of my college years was more traumatic.

It was early evening on a Saturday, August 12, 1995. I was visiting my parents in Pasadena for the weekend and had just returned to their house after being out all day. A month before, my dad had earned his doctor of missiology degree from Fuller. Now my parents were in the final stages of planning a return to India to launch a program for tribal people there. I had spoken to my mom that morning and knew they were planning to join friends for dinner.

I noticed the light on the answering machine blinking red. The message was alarming: "This is Huntington Hospital. We are trying to reach the son of P. V. and Jolly Joseph. Please call us."

Deeply concerned, I immediately returned the call and was told, "You need to come in. Your parents have been in an accident."

I pressed for more information even though I was afraid to hear the answer: "Are they okay?"

After a moment's hesitation, the woman on the other line gently responded. "Your dad is in the ICU. But I'm sorry to say that your mom passed away."

In shock, I hung up the phone and stood there, unable to move or breathe.

No. This can't be. There's no way this can be real. There must be a mistake.

I later learned a woman had driven through a red light and smashed her Chevy Suburban into the side of my parents' Nissan sedan. Dad suffered significant internal injuries. Mom was declared dead at the hospital.

Those next two weeks of dealing with the grief, family and friends, a funeral and memorial service, and my dad's hospital care were a blur. Losing Mom was devastating. I'd always been close to her. Now I felt that the anchor of my life had been ripped away.

After about six months, my dad recovered from his physical injuries and decided to move back to India. I knew I should finish my undergraduate degree at Azusa, but then what? I decided to postpone any thoughts of graduate school. I needed a break. It was a difficult, uncertain time.

After graduating from Azusa Pacific, I took a job at a USC research lab while I tried to figure out my future. I thought I might want to pursue a career in biomedical research. Always in the back of my mind, however, was the documentary I'd seen of the Japanese doctor in China and the idea of helping people with medical needs in underdeveloped nations.

After two years I left the research lab to enter graduate school at Loma Linda University. Thanks in part to the encouragement of my best friend, I decided to pursue a master's degree in public health rather than medical research. My focus at Loma Linda was originally on biostatistics. When I began a master's internship overseas, however, I finally found the path that truly resonated with my heart.

I was back in India, serving for three months in a rural area near the town of Jamkhed in the state of Maharashtra. There I saw the dramatic effects one doctor and a little health education could have on a community. It might have been only routine checkups and asking a few simple questions—"Are your kids healthy? Have you followed up on the nutrition lesson we talked about last time?"—combined with a brief exam. Yet for most people in these villages, it was so much more medical attention than they were accustomed to.

I saw that a small medical facility, coupled with a strong community health education program, led to positive, long-term changes. Our influence went beyond medical considerations. When we treated villagers with courtesy and kindness, it generated smiles. We could see the people felt valued. When we left them, they felt better, not just physically but also mentally, emotionally, and spiritually.

Then there was the social impact. Even today, many people in India look down on members of what are considered the lower castes. When we provided medical training to villagers who were part of these lower castes, it raised their status in the community and empowered them. People of the higher castes now had to go to and learn from these villagers if they wanted to improve their health.

Those three months near Jamkhed changed my life. I saw how I could make a difference in the world. The connection to my childhood dream was complete. My mom had always encouraged me to pursue a career in medicine. By combining my master's degree in international public health with a medical degree, I could honor those wishes and fulfill the purpose I was now certain I'd been born for. For the first time since my mother's death, I was excited about the future.

I began a medical program in Cambridge, England. At the same time, despite the challenges of living thousands of miles apart, my relationship with Cilicia grew deeper and stronger. On August 17, 2002, in front of nearly three hundred family and friends and with Cilicia's father officiating, we said our wedding vows and committed our lives to each other.

Now, ten years and four kids later, I was enjoying life with my family in Colorado Springs. I scooped Eshaan off the floor and carried him upstairs. After a quick diaper change, I slipped him into a fresh onesie and his tiny sleeping bag—the white one with multicolored letters of the alphabet on it—and walked into the bedroom he shared with his sister. I turned off the light.

Eshaan yawned as I cradled him in my arms. Silently I offered up his good-night prayer: *God, please be with Eshaan while I'm away. Protect him and mold him for your purposes and plans for his life. Be with us both until we meet again.*

I didn't want to lay him down just yet. Instead, I studied Eshaan's face in the shadows, absorbing every feature: his tiny nose and mouth, the dark hair on his head, his brown eyes, already heavy and ready to close. I wanted to memorize this precious image.

How much will he change in the month I'll be gone? How will he react when I return? Will he recognize me? I hadn't left yet, and I missed him already.

Reluctantly I laid Eshaan in his crib and gently kissed him on his forehead. I'd given my heart to this little guy, just as I'd given it to his sister and brothers, to his mother, and to the nation I now called home. Another country was calling me, however, a country that had also earned a piece of my heart.

I wondered what adventures awaited Eshaan. His journey was only just beginning. I realized I would have to wait to find out. It was time to continue my own journey.

AFGHANISTAN

4:30 P.M., THURSDAY, NOVEMBER 29, 2012
KABUL, AFGHANISTAN

THE SUN WAS ALREADY LOW IN THE SKY WHEN MY AIRBUS JET dipped its wings for its approach into Kabul. Since we'd left Dubai two hours before, I'd enjoyed conversing with my seatmates—a French photojournalist and an Afghan rug salesman. From my spot between these two travelers, I leaned toward the window to catch a glimpse of the city that had become almost a second home.

So much had changed in the four years since my first trip here. The nation's capital was heavily populated then, but Kabul and the surrounding area had increased to a population of five million. Roads, buildings, and businesses had all expanded. It was gradually becoming a thriving metropolis.

My perspective of Afghanistan and its people had changed a great deal as well. I had been excited on that first trip but also nervous. I wondered: *Would the people accept me? Could I contribute here? Was this my future?*

The trip had come together in a hurry. My family and I had moved back to the States in 2007 so I could complete my doctor of medicine degree and join an American residency program. At the end of that year, Cilicia had started a job in Colorado Springs as a strategy analyst with Compassion International, an organization dedicated to helping children living in poverty.

More than a year later, however, I was still looking for the right position for me. One night, as I stood in the back of a room and watched a presentation about humanitarian work overseas, a balding, broad-shouldered man with a quiet voice approached me. "Hey, I've heard about you," he said. "It would be great if we could get together sometime and get to know each other."

The man, Daniel, was president of Morning Star Development. We met soon after, and I felt an instant connection with him. When I described what I hoped to focus on in my career—preventive and clinical medicine, international public health, humanitarian work, and teaching—he leaned back and smiled.

"Those are the exact things we're looking for in a medical director," he said.

Daniel was leaving for Afghanistan in two weeks. He invited me to join him and see what their work was all about.

When I got home from the meeting, I said to Cilicia, "Guess what? I might have a job." Then I explained that there was one tiny hitch.

"If I took this position and ended up making medical training trips to Afghanistan," I said, "how would you feel about that? Would you have any hesitations or security concerns?"

Cilicia has an amazing, strong spiritual faith. She didn't even blink. "If this is what you are supposed to do," she said, "I think security would be the least of my worries." Despite the violent history of Afghanistan, I felt the same way. I accepted Daniel's offer to join him on the trip.

Even though I'd grown up in that region of the world, there was so much about this nation I didn't know. My research showed that Afghanistan was about the size of Texas, but that was where any similarity with the Lone Star State ended. Afghanistan's population of twenty-eight million[1] was 99 percent Muslim.[2] Two-thirds of the population were illiterate.[3] The average lifespan was forty-three years;[4] more than a tenth of the nation's children did not even reach the age of five.[5] To offset meager incomes, many Afghans turned to cultivating poppy fields—the country was the world's foremost producer of opium, the key ingredient for heroin.[6]

I wondered what I was getting myself into.

Two weeks later, with the morning sun just beginning to slant red-hued rays across the landscape below, I got my first glimpse of the towering, snow-capped peaks that surround Kabul. The highest point in the Hindu Kush is at an elevation of nearly twenty-five thousand feet; Kabul sits at nearly six thousand feet. The view from my plane window reminded me of Denver and the Rocky Mountains, though these peaks are even more prominent. As we flew over the city, I was surprised to see that Kabul was laid out in a well-planned grid, including a downtown, rows of residential houses, and a business district.

The picture was a bit different on the ground, however. After connecting with my driver, I was soon hurtling through potholed streets in what felt like a high-speed car chase. At each major intersection, we raced into a roundabout filled with cars, trucks, bicyclists, and pedestrians jockeying for position, always within inches of each other. In the middle of it all, a lone policeman holding an AK-47 stood on a small concrete platform and watched over us.

Those policemen weren't the only signs that I was now in a war zone. Armed Afghan soldiers in green-and-brown camouflage uniforms patrolled the streets. Nearly every dilapidated home and building were protected by brick walls at least ten feet high and lined with razor wire. Everything was covered with layers of mud. The citizens of Kabul, however, appeared to take these conditions in stride. Women wearing headscarves bartered over fruits and vegetables with shopkeepers whose tiny storefronts lined dirty, cluttered sidewalks. Men in groups of two or three—most of the older ones in traditional garb and many of the younger ones in Western-style jackets and pants—dodged traffic on the way to their destinations.

At last we arrived at the locked gate and modest home of our NGO team house. I met the staff and was soon ushered into a meeting with members of another NGO. They were leaving the country and wanted to know if Morning Star would take over their medical clinic. It was fascinating to hear what was being done to help and equip the Afghan people, medically and otherwise—and to hear how much more help was needed.

One of the visiting team members that morning was Cheryl Beckett, a thirty-year-old Ohio native who'd helped feed and give medical assistance to Afghans for the previous five years. Little did I know that we would strike up a friendship on my successive trips—or that seventeen months later, she would be among ten volunteers massacred, reportedly by the Taliban, on the way back to Kabul after an aid mission.*

It was the next morning that I met Rafiq, program director for three of the NGO's community centers. If I did join Morning Star, this was a man I would work with closely, so I hoped to make a good impression.

Rafiq was nearly six feet tall and, unlike most Afghans, clean

---

*Multiple Taliban groups claimed responsibility for the killings.

shaven and wearing a dress shirt and jeans. We sat on couches in the team house living room and made small talk. I learned that Rafiq was in his early thirties, was a well-respected member of a tribe in the nation's eastern provinces, and had earned a medical degree and completed a public health internship. He had a wife and three children.

I realized that his background wasn't so different from mine. I was ashamed to think I'd anticipated someone a bit narrow-minded, with limited education or understanding of world affairs. Rafiq, however, was intelligent, knowledgeable, fluent in English, and passionate about his work. He was so accomplished, in fact, that an international organization in Afghanistan would later nominate him for the 2013 Nobel Peace Prize for his contributions to the nation's rural communities.

It would not be the last time I'd have to adjust my thinking in this surprising country.

That afternoon I met Rafiq's driver and assistant, Farzad. He was in his late forties, about five inches shorter than Rafiq, with a more typical Afghan appearance—full beard and adorned in the long, loose shirt with pajama-like trousers known as the *salwar kameez*. Farzad greeted me with a "Hello, sir, how are you?" though I soon learned his English did not go much further than this. He was always smiling and extremely friendly, even stopping to pat dogs as they ambled by.

Later that week I traveled out of the city for the first time. The occasion was the dedication of the Pul-i-assim Community Center. Morning Star had received permission from the area's tribal elders to operate the center, giving people a place to come for medical care and training as well as education. It served more than fifty surrounding villages, including four thousand children.

On the drive out of Kabul, I expected to find a countryside devastated by war. Except for Afghan National Army patrols, however, I observed no evidence of conflict. Instead, I took in views of wheat and rice fields as well as orchards of apricot, plum, and apple trees.

We were still on the paved section of the Kabul-Jalalabad Highway when our driver slowed. I saw, ahead of us on the road, a brown, dusty cloud moving toward us on what seemed to be a million legs. We pulled off, and I watched, fascinated, as weathered men with long headscarves and walking sticks slowly guided hundreds of sheep past us and toward Kabul. These nomads, known as *Kuchis*, number more than two million people throughout Afghanistan. Revered by their countrymen for maintaining a lifestyle that Afghans had practiced for centuries, they earned their living by herding and selling sheep, goats, donkeys, and even camels.

Farther on, we reached a village with one-story adobe homes lining both sides of the highway. The homes, more like huts, were constructed of mud and sun-dried bricks made from sand, clay, water, sticks, and manure. Many of these homes featured an opening that served as a storefront. Residents attempted to catch the attention of passersby with goods such as biscuits, fruit, soda, and sugar.

In that same village we slowed nearly to a stop when we came upon a game of street soccer. Kids ranging in age from about as old as twelve to as young as two were kicking a sack cloth tied with string on the pavement. Some wore sandals while others played in bare feet. The game halted as we drove through. They watched us carefully until we'd passed, then immediately resumed the game.

Soon after, the highway pavement petered out. As the twisting dirt road led us closer to the community center, I saw more single-story adobe homes scattered on the brown, rolling hills around us. Each structure was contained by a wall of rock and mud.

At last we arrived. The community center itself was a compound that included a one-level brick-and-concrete medical clinic, an education building, and a small agricultural plot. The clinic was funded and built by a NATO-sponsored team five years before, while the education building had recently been completed with the help of Morning Star partner funds.

More than one hundred people soon gathered in the compound courtyard for the ceremony. As NGO and local officials thanked one another in speeches through a bullhorn, I stood at the edge of the crowd. I'd met a local man earlier that morning and mentioned that I was originally from India. Now this friendly fellow began speaking to me in a mix of Hindi and Urdu, two languages with which I was somewhat familiar. He was shorter than me, in his early twenties, probably a member of the Pashtun tribe from somewhere near the Pakistan border. He'd clearly taken a liking to me. He told me about some of his aspirations, including the idea of traveling to India to receive an education.

I realized once again that I'd misjudged Afghanistan and its people. I'd expected to find men and women who'd been defeated by generations of war. Instead, I encountered a young man full of dreams for the future.

After the ceremony many of us moved to the backyard of one of the village leaders. Rafiq pointed out an elder gentleman there who was breathing hard. As the foreign doctor in the crowd, I was expected to come up with a solution, so I offered to give him a brief exam. When I pulled out my stethoscope and listened, I heard mucous buildup in his lungs. I suggested a local medicine, gave him advice on steam therapy, and recommended he rub a balm on his chest before going to sleep.

It turned out that this man was the father of the local police chief. Both he and the chief were appreciative, smiling and thanking me repeatedly. Though my efforts were minimal, it was far more medical care than they were used to. I was encouraged. If even a cursory exam and a little extra attention had this kind of impact, perhaps I *could* make a difference here.

By the end of those two weeks, there was no doubt in my mind that I'd found my future. The people of Afghanistan had touched me. I told Daniel that I was ready to join the team.

On subsequent trips I grew more and more comfortable in Afghanistan. My position as medical director allowed me to teach, to treat people, and to help shape our long-term plans. It was rewarding work. I got to know the NGO staff, committed men and women from both in country and other nations. Rafiq and Farzad were among those who became trusted friends.

Though it felt right to be in Afghanistan and most of the people we served were grateful for our efforts, it was impossible to ignore signs indicating another view. The farther we traveled away from Kabul and into rural areas, where insurgent influence was far stronger, the more likely we were to see the white flag of the Taliban posted alongside a bomb crater or atop a mountain. It was a warning that we had traveled into what they considered their territory.

Once, on a trip to assess medical conditions in the eastern provinces, I rode in a car with a local colleague. He turned to me and said in English, "This area is not good. When we come to a checkpoint, please do not open your mouth. Don't say anything."

Soon after, we approached a post manned by Afghan National Army soldiers. A metal bar blocked our passage. A soldier in a camouflage uniform and holding an AK-47 stepped out of the open-air, brick structure beside the road. "Why are you traveling here?" he demanded when we stopped the car. I took my colleague's advice and let him do the talking. Though there should have been no threat from government forces, I'd seen too many signs of the Taliban presence. One can't always be sure where a stranger's sympathies lie. We were allowed to pass, but it was one of the few times I was uneasy in this nation I'd come to love.

I wasn't thinking about any of this when my plane touched down at Kabul International Airport on November 29, 2012. I'd been impatient to return. A mix-up with my visa had left me stranded in Chicago a week longer than I'd planned, delaying my arrival. Now I just wanted to get to work.

My first full day back in the country, however, involved a very different assignment. I had agreed to help judge a college debate tournament. More than twenty teams participated, each averaging about six students. They took positions on topics such as freedom and liberty in Afghanistan, women's rights within the Muslim tradition, and the right to an education.

As I listened to the students present their arguments, I was impressed by their speaking skills and the respect they showed one another. One young man in particular caught my attention. Ajmal's appearance was fashionable. He looked to be about nineteen and wore tight jeans and a checkered dress shirt. He was clean shaven, his dark hair slicked back with gel. What amazed me most, however, was his command of the English language and passion for issues that would define the next generation of this nation. Every word was distinct, and every contention was logical and clear.

If this is the future of Afghanistan, I thought, *this is a place worth investing in.*

Following the debate tournament, I spent a day of planning at the Kabul team house with Rafiq and three days with one of our teams in a northeastern province. While there, I taught a session on holistic health and enjoyed time with the directors of our leadership institute.

I returned to Kabul on December 4. By six the next morning Rafiq, Farzad, and I were on the highway. By nine we were pulling into the compound of the Pul-i-assim Community Center. More than twenty mothers and their children from neighboring villages had already gathered inside the lobby and outside the medical clinic. Some had walked thirty minutes to be there. Others had walked for five hours.

I began by checking in with the local doctor and his patients. Later I listened in on Miriam's talk about nutrition. It was here that the earnest, young mother with three children caught my eye and reminded me how important our work truly was.

By midmorning Rafiq and I were ready for a break. We walked beyond the clinic compound, taking in the austere beauty of our surroundings—to the southeast, layer upon layer of brown, rolling hills dotted by occasional clumps of green and yellow vegetation; to the south, a lush valley, including plantations filled with apricot trees and wheat and rice fields.

Suddenly I spied, across the valley, a handful of men walking our way. They were probably a half hour's distance. Two of them carried long objects that could certainly have been weapons. Earlier that morning local police had informed us of Taliban movements on the other side of the valley and advised us to proceed cautiously. We planned then to complete our work that day and return to Kabul before nightfall. I was not especially concerned. I trusted the people around me and the safety protocols we followed.

I was curious, however, about these men. I turned to Rafiq: "What do you think those guys are doing?"

"Maybe they are some Taliban and mujahideen coming to the village to ask for *Zakah.*"

The villagers were double-minded about the Taliban. Some viewed them as pure devotees of fundamental Muslim law. They even revered the insurgents. Others were less enthusiastic. The Taliban sometimes came into their villages and asked for *Zakah*—in Islamic tradition, the practice of giving from what Allah has already provided to others in "need." Of course the people gave food and money to these armed warriors even though they had very little to feed their own families. I couldn't help feeling that most donated out of a sense of intimidation and fear rather than genuine support for the Taliban cause. To me, it appeared to be more about extortion than faith.

I was offended by the idea of young men who intentionally chose the path of insurgency asking for alms. It was an injustice. When, I wondered, would this practice end in communities like this? Morning Star had been working here for seven years. The insurgency hadn't stopped. The Taliban influence continued.

I was too upset by these thoughts to continue my conversation with Rafiq. As we walked silently back to the community center, I glanced at the village schoolhouse that sat adjacent to the compound. In the previous three years insurgents had targeted both the school and the community center in attacks from neighboring mountains. On several occasions rocket-propelled grenades (RPGs) had hit the community center, shattering windows. Once, a rocket hit the side of the water tower situated on top of the health clinic. I'd been told that the insurgents wanted the school shut down, citing the usual justifications that girls did not need to be educated and a few hours a week of schooling was enough for boys.

I returned to the clinic feeling discouraged, but I'd already dismissed thoughts of the men across the valley. I trusted that we were taking adequate precautions. A personal encounter with the Taliban was the last thing on my mind.

Later that morning the local police chief invited Rafiq, Farzad, the local doctor, and me to lunch. No matter how poor or remote the village, meals in Afghanistan are always an elaborate affair. This day was no exception. At the chief's home we sat cross-legged on long cushions. On the floor in front of us lay a leather mat spread as a tablecloth. A young boy approached with a steel bowl. The bowl was placed in front of each person to catch water poured onto our outstretched hands. The routine continued until everyone seated had finished washing his hands. Given the ever-present dust in this country, the practice made perfect sense and added to the sense of hospitality that Afghans are famous for.

To my surprise, more young boys appeared, each walking in from the front door and carrying sumptuous servings: pilau rice, mutton and chicken, celery shoots, onions, and tomatoes. Everything was delicious.

Immediately after lunch our hosts served tea and pomegranates. As I cracked open and tasted my pomegranate, I realized that my skill in handling this fruit was lacking. My shirt was soon covered with red stains. If I didn't know better, I would have thought I'd just emerged from a complicated surgery. The marks on my shirt looked exactly like blood.

Once we finished eating, we talked for a few more minutes, then climbed into the Hilux for the drive back to the community center. I understood very little Pashto, and not everything was translated for me, but I gathered that part of the conversation was about security. Only months later did I learn about some of the questions raised at this time: Should we wait for an escort before driving back? Should we wait for approval from the district police chief?

At the time, Rafiq did tell me that the village police chief said, "Why don't you spend the night?" It was customary in Afghanistan to invite guests to stay for the next meal and then spend the night, so I didn't place any extra meaning behind his request. I didn't connect it to concerns over our safety. Rafiq and I politely turned down his invitation. The others decided it was safe for my colleagues and me to begin our journey back up the mountain road to Kabul.

At about two thirty we dropped off the chief and local doctor at the community center, said our good-byes, and headed out of the village. Rafiq drove faster than usual.

I still felt frustrated over my earlier conversation with Rafiq about the Taliban practice of intimidating the villagers and asking them to give up their precious resources. When talk in the pickup turned again to the insurgents, I said, "Man, if these guys want so badly to be involved in the community, maybe we should just give them the community center and let them handle it."

I didn't mean it. I knew that Taliban fundamentalism had taken what was a stable and prosperous nation in the 1960s and 70s back to medieval times. I certainly didn't wish for the Taliban to control the people in the villages even more. I was simply angry at the situation.

Rafiq and Farzad were silent.

It was only a few minutes later that my anger at these unseen extremists turned to shock over confronting them in person. As men holding AK-47s forced me to march up the hill toward more armed insurgents, one question pounded in my mind like a sledgehammer. It was a question I was afraid to answer.

Am I about to die?

ANGUISH AND PEACE

3:50 P.M., WEDNESDAY, DECEMBER 5
MOUNTAIN RANGE EAST OF KABUL, AFGHANISTAN
MY HEART WAS HEAVY AS I TRIED TO KEEP MY BALANCE ON
the steep and winding mountain trail. With my hands tied behind
me, it wasn't easy.

Rafiq, Farzad, and I, along with our four Taliban captors, had
been hiking single file up the mountain for twenty minutes. The
men I'd spotted above us when we began the hike had just joined us.
Now we were outnumbered seven to three. Each kidnapper carried
a Kalashnikov. Whenever my gait slowed too much for the liking of
the captor behind me, I felt the barrel of his weapon nudge me in the
back.

The weather did not match the desperation I felt. It was a sunny day,
a comfortable fifty-plus degrees. The terrain, however, was desolate—
dusty and rocky, the predominant colors gray and brown. I saw no
trees, only a few green *shamshoby* shrubs attempting to add life to our
sparse surroundings. The mountains loomed over us, stretching to the
horizon in an uneven and endless pattern.

I noticed up ahead, to the left of our trail, a break in the bleakness around us—a pool of water, nearly three feet in diameter. Rafiq, in front of me, called out in Pashto, "Could we have a drink?"

The kidnapper who'd driven the commandeered Hilux, apparently the group's leader, raised his hand. Everyone stopped. Our hands were untied—thankfully, they remained untied for the rest of our captivity.

A gunman motioned us toward the pool.

Rafiq and Farzad, along with some of our captors, cupped their hands in the cool water and drank. My medical background made me more cautious, however. I did not want to be hiking and dealing with diarrhea from an unwelcome parasite. I chose not to drink, a decision I would come to regret.

After another few minutes of hiking, we stopped again. This time the leader demanded that I hand over my backpack. He had a knife tucked into his waistband. I couldn't see the blade, but from the size of the curved hilt, it must have been huge. Only later did I learn that this man had participated in multiple kidnappings and beheaded many of his captives. His nickname was the "Butcher."

After rifling through my backpack during our initial confrontation, our captors had returned it to me for the hike. Now they wanted a closer look. My heart sank when the Butcher pulled out my passport. Though I had no need to bring it to the clinic, I'd forgotten to take it out before leaving Kabul that morning. My hopes of being mistaken for a traveler from India were gone. There was no hiding the prominent *United States of America* typed next to my photo.

The Butcher held out my passport to another captor, saying what must have been something like, "Look, American." The man next to him examined the passport closely.

To my surprise, however, my captors seemed even more intrigued by a booklet of family pictures. Cilicia had put together a mini album of photos after a recent visit with my father and given it to me for the trip. Now the kidnappers looked closely at each image and through Rafiq's translation asked me about them: "Is this your wife? Are these your children? Who is this man?"

Their intense interest could be at least partly explained by Afghan culture. Pashtuns are the largest ethnic group in the country, comprising roughly 40 percent of its people.[1] They are fiercely loyal to family and tribe. They think of themselves primarily not as Muslims or Afghans but as members and representatives of their extended families and the people who make up their tribe. In Afghanistan, to understand another's family is to understand that person at the core.

The gunmen had already taken my cell phone during their first search. Now, after also removing my passport, the Butcher returned the backpack to me. It was time to move on.

One of my original captors—the tall one who sat with the leader in the Hilux—had not joined in the latest examination of my backpack. As we walked, he pointed to Rafiq and asked me, "Is he the *ferengi* [foreigner]?"

Clearly these men had been looking specifically for me, the American. Someone had alerted them about our visit to the village.

"Nay, nay," I said in answer to the question about Rafiq. "Jalalabad *wallah* [That guy's from the Jalalabad area]."

If there had been any remaining confusion among the kidnappers about which of us didn't belong here, it was erased now.

A half hour later, we reached a plateau at the highest peak in the area. From there we could see miles of hills and looked down into one brown valley after another.

I wasn't enjoying the scenery, however. I strained to spy a compound or hut, anything that might signify the presence of human life. I was crestfallen when I realized there was nothing out there. We were alone in the middle of nowhere.

Is this it? Are they going to shoot us now and roll our bodies down this hill?

Our captors, instead, spread out a blanket, sat down, and produced a loaf of naan, the local bread. Apparently it was time for a snack break.

The Butcher motioned for Rafiq, Farzad, and me to sit also. He offered each of us a piece of naan. Since the three of us were still full from the feast at the police chief's house, however, we all politely declined. As our kidnappers continued to talk, I wondered if they were deciding when and where to dispose of us.

Then it was time for *namaz*, or prayer. Two of our captors took off their headscarves and laid them on the ground. Then four of them dropped to their knees, all apparently facing Mecca, and began the Muslim ritual of bowing, chanting, and praying.

Anger surged through me. *How can they pray to Allah when they are holding hostages at gunpoint just a few feet away? If Allah is merciful and just, as the Koran says, how is this action merciful and just?*

Their passion for their spiritual beliefs was clear, but I struggled to see how it connected to a life-giving faith. It seemed to me that these men were more willing to take life than give it. They believed that killing others was their only path to salvation. I felt it was an example of traditionalism, a dead faith of the living, rather than tradition, a living faith passed on by one's ancestors.

And yet my own faith and upbringing demanded that I not judge these men. I knew nothing about their backgrounds, nothing about the experiences that had led them to this point. As tempted as I was to give in to anger and even hate, I sensed in that moment that I needed to adopt a different attitude.

Can I do it? Can I show them compassion, even love, despite what I'm feeling right now? I wondered if I would even get the chance.

From my spot on the ground, just a few feet from the circle of kidnappers, I tried to speak as inconspicuously as possible to Rafiq: "Do you have any idea what they might be thinking?"

His whispered reply was so soft I could barely make it out: "No idea." Then he offered some advice: "If they ask if you are a Christian, just tell them you're a Hindu."

I hadn't even contemplated this potential dilemma yet. If asked, would I deny my faith, or would I stand up for my beliefs and perhaps be executed on the spot? Under the circumstances this didn't seem the time to start a discussion about it. I whispered back, "Okay, okay."

Once our captors finished their prayers, they talked among themselves a few more minutes. Then four of them marched down a side trail, leaving three Taliban with the three of us. I am not a violent person, nor am I trained in any kind of hand-to-hand combat, but for the briefest of moments I thought we might have a chance to surprise them and escape. Then I remembered they all had guns while we had nothing.

Two of the three remaining captors were part of the group that initially abducted us—the tall one, whom I began to think of as "the Hopeless guy" because of the forlorn expression that was always on his face, and the stocky, younger insurgent the others called Ahmed.

The new member of the group seemed to be in charge now. He had fairer skin than the rest and held his left arm out stiffly, as if it were frozen in place. They called this one Haqqani, apparently because he'd been trained in Pakistan. It also might have been because he was part of the Haqqani network, the insurgent group believed to be based in Pakistan near the Afghan border. Founded by Jalaluddin Haqqani, once an ally of the United States and a trusted associate of Osama bin Laden, the network was tied to both the Taliban and al-Qaeda. Its members were reportedly responsible for multiple kidnappings, assassination attempts, and some of the most audacious attacks in Afghanistan, including assaults on hotels, the 2008 bombing of the Indian Embassy in Kabul, a 2011 attack on the U.S. Embassy, and several attempted truck bombings.

Jalaluddin Haqqani was in fact the original link between the Taliban and what became al-Qaeda. Bin Laden joined Haqqani in 1984 to provide funds and engineering advice for his operations. They developed a close friendship. When bin Laden founded al-Qaeda in 1988, he established his first training camp in the mountains of Afghanistan's Khost province, on the border with Pakistan and Haqqani's homeland. The Taliban then hosted bin Laden and his al-Qaeda training camps for years.

I did not want to think about how the Haqqani with us now might be connected to this dark history. With a frown, this Haqqani told us to get up. It was again time to walk.

Step after step after step. At least I was in decent shape. Back home I played an occasional set of tennis and often took afternoon walks along the trails near my workplace. Even so, I now struggled to keep up and often fell to the back of our procession—or nearly so, as Haqqani always brought up the rear. He continued to let me know when he felt my pace was too slow by a poke in the back with his AK-47.

I did have comfortable footwear—Faded Glory walking shoes I'd purchased at a Wal-Mart. Farzad, in tennis shoes, and Rafiq, in dress shoes, seemed to be keeping up fine. The Taliban were all fit and moved at a steady rate. Each wore American-style tennis shoes that reminded me of Converse.

No one spoke as the minutes and miles passed. It gave me a chance, for the first time, to gather my thoughts, really consider where I was and what was happening. Nothing focuses your thoughts quite like the expectation that you will be killed in the next few hours or even moments.

What, I wondered, had I truly accomplished in my life to this point? Had I had the kind of effect that would be remembered by anyone besides my family and a few friends? What kind of legacy would I leave behind, especially to my children?

I pictured my family's faces: beautiful Cilicia, Asha, Jaron, Tobi, and little Eshaan. I'd spent enough time with each of my three eldest children to get to know them and their personalities. They would remember me, at least, if I died today. But Eshaan?

Unlike his brothers, Eshaan had been calm and quiet when he was born, more like his sister. There was something comforting about his demeanor right from the beginning. The name we chose for him had special meaning. In Arabic and Egyptian, *Ishaan* means "guidance and direction." For me, it was a way to commemorate the work I did among Muslims in Afghanistan. Additionally, in Sanskrit *Eshwar* translates to "Almighty God." I felt that in this combination of names, we were honoring the work that God would do in Eshaan's life.

Now I wondered if I would miss it all.

Thinking about Eshaan pierced my soul in a way that nothing else could. I choked back a sob. *Eshaan, you are so young. I'm so sorry that you may have to grow up without a father. I am so sorry.*

That moment of lonely anguish was one of the lowest of my life. Strangely, however, it also became the moment when my attitude began to shift.

Yes, I have been kidnapped by the Taliban. Yes, I am marching deeper into a remote Afghan mountain range with a gun at my back, almost certain to die soon. But I do not want to die a victim.

It's no one else's doing that you're here right now, I tell myself. *You made this choice. You've always known about the risk. You do this work for a reason.*

My father, a church historian, taught me a story in my youth that came to mind at this moment. In an ancient Babylonian kingdom three young Jewish refugees refused to bow down and worship a statue erected by the king. When the king threatened them with execution in a fiery furnace, they replied, "If we are thrown into the blazing furnace, the God we serve is able to save us from it, and he will rescue us from your hand, O king. But even if he does not, we want you to know, O king, that we will not serve your gods or worship the image of gold you have set up."[2] The king had the three tossed in the furnace, but after a few minutes all three emerged unharmed.

Wow! I think. *That is a solid faith. They believed completely that God would be with them even in that furnace.*

Well, the God of those three young men is walking with me right now too. These could be my last hours. I don't want to regret how I handle this. If I am going to die here, I want to thank God through it all. I want to express my faith and gratitude in a way that will have a lasting, positive impact. Others may have reason to gripe, but I don't. I have so much to be grateful for.

In my mind I begin to list the highlights of my life. Growing up in a family that taught me to reach out and help make life better for others. Moving to the States. Completing high school, college, and graduate school. Traveling to many countries and experiencing many different cultures. Joining Morning Star and having the opportunity to bring medical help and training to Afghans. Marrying Cilicia and beginning to raise my own family.

You know what? That's a pretty good life. A full life.

The more I thought about it, the more I realized how truly blessed I was. I still had hope and peace. Could my Taliban kidnappers say that?

I wondered what these men thought as they observed me. *If I am the book these guys are going to read, what is being written in this chapter? What are they reading in me right now? If I've been put in this situation to show them another approach to life, how do I reflect that? Certainly not with anxiety, tension, and uncertainty.* I sensed that I was being challenged.

As I trudged farther with each step from the life I knew and the people I loved, I was thankful that the God I knew seemed to be allowing me to see the bigger picture—that he was still in charge and that I still had a role to play, even in what might be my final moments. I was okay. Even here, now, I could choose to find peace.

The sun was setting, sending slivers of uneven shadows across our path, when another childhood memory came to mind. It was a tune I'd sung hundreds of times without thinking much about the meaning of the words. Now, however, those words meant everything to me. In my mind I started singing it over and over, sometimes alternating it with another song, but always coming back to the original. Twice, caught up in my emotions, I had to clamp my mouth shut as I began to sing out loud: "Jesus, name above all names . . ."

As the darkness spread, I concentrated my eyes on the narrow trail so I wouldn't stumble or fall. My head was lowered, but my heart was in the heavens.

TALIBAN HOSPITALITY

CHAPTER FOUR

7:15 P.M., WEDNESDAY

I NEVER EVEN NOTICED THE DEPRESSION IN THE TRAIL. WHEN my left leg slipped into the hole, I was too tired to respond. My ankle twisted. I tripped and landed on my left knee and hand, narrowly avoiding tumbling headlong into the dirt. As tempted as I was to let myself fall so I could just lie there, I knew that wasn't an option. Haqqani's Kalashnikov nudged me even as I staggered to my feet.

Four hours. That's how long we'd been hiking with almost no break at all. Fatigue, mixed with a rise in altitude and adrenaline spikes and drops from facing armed kidnappers, had begun to wear me down. Rafiq also seemed to be moving slower. I had to admire Farzad and our captors, however. They still seemed to be pushing forward with relative ease.

Passing clouds partly obscured the two-thirds-full moon. My eyes had mostly adjusted to the darkness, but my feet did not always cooperate. The fall was my second since sundown. Fortunately my ankle seemed all right. And I didn't feel so bad about it when Hopeless also tripped and nearly sprawled on the trail a few minutes after I did.

37

A half hour earlier I'd spotted a single-story structure on a hill, ahead and to the left of the direction we were headed. Though I didn't see light or movement, it immediately raised my hopes. What if people saw the six of us walking in the dark? Would they stop us and ask questions? Would the sight of guns scare them off, or would they decide to get involved?

Unfortunately, our captors led us on into the night without even a glance at the home on the hill. It was another letdown on a day over-flowing with extreme emotions.

A few minutes later Rafiq's voice broke the stillness. Though I didn't know what he'd said in Pashto, I soon understood when our captors stopped and Rafiq sat down. Grateful for the respite, I plopped down near my friend. The three gunmen soon joined us on the ground.

This was a rare opportunity to catch my breath and gather my thoughts. *Man, I need to find a way to identify with these guys. No matter how different we are, there must be a way.*

Inspiration struck a moment later. I whisper to Rafiq, "Should I tell them that my kids have Pashtun blood?"

He considers this a moment; then without looking at me whispers back, "Go ahead."

I clear my throat and begin to speak in a loud voice: "I just want you to know that I am originally from India. And as such, I am your neighbor."

Each of the three Taliban watch me closely as I speak. I see no anger or malice in their eyes, but there is nothing encouraging there either. I keep going, as Rafiq continues translating for me.

"Historically, India has been a big-brother nation to Afghanistan. If not for the political boundaries drawn by the British close to a century ago in your land, we would all still be one nation."

Still no response. I'm glad for the pause while Rafiq translates my words. It gives me time to decide what to say next.

"I also have the privilege of having Pashtun blood in my family," I say. "My wife's great, great, paternal grandmother was a Pashtun princess who married a man from India. So my children have some Pashtun blood in them as a result.

"I have come to your nation several times now with the hope of being of assistance in the rebuilding of your nation. My desire is to continue the same great relationship that our countrymen have had for a very long time."

My speech was over. I was disappointed by the lack of response. The three Taliban made no comments and asked no questions. What had I expected? I suppose I'd hoped for something along the line of, "Sorry, we didn't realize you are one of us. You can go now."

Obviously that wasn't going to happen.

Nevertheless, it felt good to have at least attempted to connect and make peace with them. I had put it out there for them to deal with. The response was now up to them.

Our hike continued, our group in the usual sequence: Ahmed led, with Rafiq just behind him. Twenty feet behind them were Farzad and Hopeless. After another twenty feet, Haqqani and I brought up the rear.

With the sun down, I had lost my sense of direction, but there was no hesitation on the part of our captors. We moved steadily, even urgently, toward what was to me an unknown destination.

It's interesting how the mind works when it is calm. Even in dire circumstances, once you've resolved that you don't need to be anxious about what's happening—in other words, once you've shut down fight-or-flight responses—the parasympathetic nervous system kicks in so your body can relax and conserve energy.

Strangely, perhaps, this was happening to me. I was pleased to notice that despite the continuous walking up and down hills and the presence of a gunman at my back, my heart was not beating at a rapid pace. For the moment, I had accepted that there was nothing I could do about the situation. It had become a routine. I wasn't consciously thinking about the danger. Even in the dark my focus was simply on placing one foot where the other foot had just been and repeating the process.

It was about an hour after my brief speech that I was startled by movement on our left. I was amazed to see it was a boy, about seven years old, forty feet away and on an intersecting course with our path. The moonlight revealed a slim youth with unruly dark hair, covered with dust. He carried three or four loaves of freshly baked naan and a kettle of water.

Where had he come from? Was it a coincidence, or had he been told to be in this exact spot at this exact time?

When the boy was close, Hopeless spoke to him. Without a word the boy handed over his load and quickly disappeared. It angered me that the Taliban had so much control over this child and his life. Yet it was an all-too-common story.

The father of the Taliban movement was a veteran of the mujahideen war against the Soviet Union, a Pashtun and Muslim fundamentalist named Mohammed Omar. In 1994, following the withdrawal of Soviet troops after its failed occupation, Afghanistan had descended into lawlessness and civil war. One day Omar was stopped and robbed by armed bandits at five roadblocks on a twenty-five-mile road between his village and Kandahar, the country's second-largest city.

Omar was outraged. He organized a *Jirga*, or tribal council, of more than fifty area religious leaders. These men formed a militia with the goal of eliminating one checkpoint. When their lightly armed party chased off the bandits without a shot being fired, they advanced to the next checkpoint. Within a week all the roadblocks between Omar's village and Kandahar had been cleared. Omar used the Pashto word for "students of Islam" to name his group: *Taliban*.

Soon after, Omar reportedly led thirty men armed with sixteen rifles to free two teenage girls who had been kidnapped and raped by a warlord, hanging the local commander from the barrel of a tank gun. More incidents like these led to support from a population weary of chaos and random violence.

Then Omar claimed to have had a dream telling him that Allah had chosen him to bring peace to Afghanistan. He found a ready supply of recruits for his new movement in madrassas—Islamic religious schools. When millions of Afghans fled their homes during the war against the Soviet Union, many ended up in refugee camps along the Afghanistan-Pakistan border. The young students here were taught a particularly austere and rigid form of Islam. They faced monotony and filth daily, with little promise for change. By comparison, Omar and the Taliban appeared to offer a life of excitement, hope, and meaning.

If the boy I'd just seen and others like him joined the Taliban, however, what hope did they really have? The Taliban may have brought order to Afghanistan, but their strict interpretation of Sharia law, brutal treatment of women, and dependence on violence to achieve their aims hardly seemed life-giving. I imagined that new converts would live not a life of peace but one of continuing aggression and terrorism. I was a doctor, trying to better equip people to deal with their medical issues. How did kidnapping or killing me foster anything that could be called peace?

After the boy left, Hopeless removed the checkered scarf that was wrapped like a turban around his head and spread it out on the trail. Haqqani placed the boy's water kettle in the middle and motioned for us to sit around it on the edge of the scarf. At least, it appeared, I would not die hungry.

The three Taliban sat opposite Rafiq, Farzad, and me so we faced one another in a tight circle. Hopeless then removed the cloth that covered a still-warm loaf of naan, tore off a chunk, and passed it on. Each of us in turn tore off a piece.

After a couple minutes of chewing, Hopeless looks at me and says via Rafiq's translation, "Isn't this the best naan you've ever tasted? This naan is even better than what's served in the best restaurants in Kabul."

I sense that Hopeless isn't just making conversation. There is almost a challenge in his voice.

"Oh, this is so good," I say. "Thank you very much."

It *was* good, and I was genuinely grateful to stop and eat after so much walking. I also did not want to disagree or say anything that might offend these men.

It was strange to be sitting so close to Taliban warriors in these remote mountains and having an almost-cordial conversation. There was no talk of violence or of how we might be killed. Our captors talked instead about their life in the mountains. It was almost as if a group of old and new friends had gathered to share a meal.

My experience has shown me that hospitality is important to us humans. We will go to great lengths to make our guests feel welcome. When I was growing up in India—perhaps the same age as the boy who had carried the naan—my parents and I went to visit a family whose father was dying of a chronic illness. The family had little; they barely could keep their roof together. While some of her children greeted us at the door, the family's mother dashed out a back door. Understanding what was happening, my parents rushed in and tried to stop the mother, but they were too late.

The mother returned a few minutes later with a package of biscuits she'd purchased. Though she clearly could not afford to do so, this poor woman felt a strong obligation to treat us well.

Hospitality is equally important, if not more so, in Afghan culture—even, it seemed, among the Taliban. Nearly all Taliban are ethnic Pashtuns. The Pashtun people adhere to a code of conduct known as *Pashtunwali*. According to the code, it is a matter of honor to take care of one's guests. Custom dictates that even an enemy, if he comes to your door and asks for refuge, must be protected as if he is a member of the family. An Afghan proverb states, "Honor the guest, O son. Even though he be an infidel, open the door."

Rafiq, Farzad, and I now benefited from this practice. Though we were prisoners and though I, as an American, represented the "enemy," they still were expected to sit down and break bread with us. It was a bit of comfort at a time when any positive sign was welcome. When no one was looking, I stuffed a piece of naan into my pocket. If I survived this ordeal, I wanted a token to remember this moment, a small piece of evidence that I had been treated well.

The naan helped fill my stomach, but I was desperately thirsty. Had I known we would be hiking for so long, I certainly would have made an effort at our first stop to screen out any nasty parasites and drunk heartily from the pool. While we ate, I eagerly kept my eye on the boy's water kettle.

Soon each of the three Taliban picked up the kettle in turn and took a long gulp from the wide opening on top. When Ahmed offered it to me, I gratefully and carefully lifted the kettle above my head and poured water into my mouth from the spout. I didn't want to miss a drop and, still concerned about parasites, also wanted to avoid putting my mouth on the kettle itself.

I was startled by a burst of laughter and comments from all three of my captors. Apparently the sight of this foreigner and his strange method of drinking water amused them greatly. A little sheepishly, I grinned back at them. It was embarrassing to be the butt of a joke but also encouraging. For those few seconds, at least, I felt they weren't looking at me as an enemy or a piece of property. We'd made another unexpected human connection.

Though it seemed unlikely, I desperately hoped that these men would allow me to also connect again with the people I cared about most.

BAD NEWS

CHAPTER FIVE

9:10 A.M., WEDNESDAY
COLORADO SPRINGS, COLORADO

AFGHANISTAN IS ELEVEN AND A HALF HOURS AHEAD OF Mountain Standard Time. At nearly the same moment I was drinking from a water kettle in front of my three Taliban captors, my boss, Daniel, was at his desk in his second-floor office at Morning Star in Colorado Springs. He jotted down a few notes, items he planned to bring up at the staff meeting later that morning.

The phone rang. It was Roy, Morning Star's director of operations in Kabul.

"Daniel, I need to let you know that Grace and I were supposed to have dinner with Dilip at five tonight," Roy said. "We hadn't heard anything from Dilip or Rafiq and had been trying to reach them for over two hours. Then, a few minutes ago, a cousin of Rafiq's came to the door. He just left. He says his family received word from someone in Pul-i-assim that Dilip, Rafiq, and Farzad were kidnapped by the Taliban."

Daniel closed his eyes.

"None of that is official," Roy said. "I haven't been contacted by

45

the Taliban or anyone else. It's still possible that they've been detained by someone, and this is just a misunderstanding. I don't know any more than that at this point."

"Okay," Daniel said. "I'm about to go into a meeting. Let's plan to talk after I'm out about how we can respond and about setting up a crisis management team."

After hanging up the phone, Daniel stared out his window, seeing but not seeing his view of undeveloped hills and, in the distance, upscale homes set amid a thick green growth of Ponderosa Pines.

Okay, what does this mean? That their vehicle broke down somewhere and they don't have cell phone coverage. Or that they've been temporarily detained.

Or that they really have been kidnapped.

There weren't many other options.

Daniel wondered if he should alert his staff at the meeting in a few minutes. *No*, he decided. *We don't have enough information yet. There's no reason to get the rumor mill started.*

He sighed as he got up from his desk. He'd always believed that if anything like this were to happen to someone at Morning Star, it would happen to him. To hear that colleagues and friends might be in mortal danger was a terrible feeling.

His mind was already racing ahead to potential responses. Without any word from the missing staff members or the supposed kidnappers, however, there was little he could do.

I hope they're okay, Daniel thought. *I just hope they're okay.*

"WE'RE GOING TO KILL YOU"

CHAPTER SIX

10:00 P.M., WEDNESDAY

MOUNTAIN RANGE EAST OF KABUL, AFGHANISTAN

I COULDN'T BELIEVE THAT AFTER NEARLY SEVEN HOURS WE were still walking. My legs were so heavy, on the verge of pain. I'd noticed Rafiq struggling to catch his breath during our rare two-minute breaks, and I could even hear Haqqani breathing hard behind me. At least my eyes had adjusted to the moonlight, making it easier to avoid tripping on the trail.

Among our trio of captives only Farzad seemed unaffected by the strenuous pace. He was clearly the most fit of the three of us. He had fought with the Afghan National Army during the early years of the Soviet intervention and apparently had kept up with his physical training. I knew Farzad was a brave man. Would he attempt to escape? Only later did I learn that he was indeed watching for an opportunity to turn the tables on our kidnappers. He hoped that if he found a way to immobilize two of them, Rafiq and I would take the initiative to subdue the third.

A half hour before, another dark structure had come into view. I'd wondered if someone really lived here in the middle of nowhere.

47

I scanned it closely for any sign of light or life but saw nothing. Our captors ignored it.

I can't believe we're passing another opportunity to stop, I thought. *Why are we still walking? Where are they taking us?*

I'd made my peace with God, but the endless hike and the uncertainty over our fate were wearing me down physically and emotionally.

Now I fought to keep up with the relentless pace. Suddenly the landscape ahead of us flattened for about a hundred yards. As we stepped into this new terrain, however, I realized it was anything but even. It had furrows—a farmer had plowed this barren land and planted crops.

Someone had gone to considerable effort to bring life to this place. I remembered my conversation about *Zakah* with Rafiq. It was a shame that this farmer, whoever he was, likely had to give up a good portion of his profit to fundamentalists. I wondered what crop lay beneath my feet. I'd heard that in some cases, the Taliban didn't allow rural Afghans to grow crops at all unless they were poppies. The heroin trade was far more lucrative than wheat.

The temperature in the mountains had dropped into what felt like the midtwenties. Puffs of white floated up from my mouth with each breath. Even so, I wasn't particularly cold. Each of us, captives and kidnappers, wore the traditional *salwar kameez*, which by itself wouldn't be much protection in this weather. But I also had long johns on my legs and a black insulated jacket with a hood.

If only my legs could hold up. How long would this go on? How long would it be before Rafiq or I collapsed from exhaustion?

Another hour passed, then most of another. It must have been close to midnight when the line ahead of me suddenly halted. Rafiq, Farzad, and I sat down immediately, along with Ahmed. Hopeless, meanwhile, walked forward another thirty feet to a ledge that overlooked a valley below.

"Wallakah!" he cried. Haqqani, near me, joined in with a shout of his own. Exhausted, I closed my eyes.

Crack!

After hours of near silence the gunshot seemed deafening. Startled, I looked up at Hopeless standing on the ledge with his Kalashnikov raised in the air.

Crack!

"Wallakah!"

The shots and shouts of that one word by Hopeless and Haqqani went on for ten minutes. Clearly they were trying to signal someone. Was it one person? A gang of Taliban? An entire village? What was the plan?

Both the shouts of the Taliban and my questions went unanswered. But I was grateful for the chance to rest my weary legs. I was too tired to worry about what would happen next.

All too soon, our captors gave up on making contact with anyone. The long hike continued. We'd now been walking for nearly nine hours.

Under different circumstances the sight of soft, white moonlight blanketing these rolling hills would have conveyed a sense of serenity. My legs, however, felt anything but serene. The sensation was closer to a blaze that had ignited in the bottom of my feet and was steadily spreading to the rest of my body. I desperately yearned for a place to rest for the night.

Still, I'd survived this long. I was grateful for that.

We climbed a slope, one steeper than most we'd encountered. As I neared the crest, I noticed a one-story home on the next hill. Like the others we'd seen that night, it was dark and lifeless, apparently abandoned. I did not want to be disappointed again and refused to hope that this was our destination. My instinct was correct. We passed it by.

Fifteen minutes later, however, my self-discipline was finally rewarded. As I followed our line up a gentle rise, I saw that the landscape ahead flattened out. About a hundred yards away and twenty yards to the left sat another lonely shack. I again steeled myself against the promise of rest that this vision offered.

A moment later my mental restraint was forgotten. Ahmed, at the front of the line, veered left toward the shelter. Was this our objective? What would happen now? Was it at last time to sleep? A surprising optimism surged through me. I could not believe that these men had forced me to walk all this way only to execute me. Perhaps I would see a new day after all.

I wondered what time it was. I never wore a watch and no longer had my cell phone. As we lined up to step inside, I stole a glance at Ahmed's arm. There was just enough moonlight for me to make out the position of the hands on his wristwatch: 12:30. Then we entered.

The shack was a room about eight by twelve feet, made of stones and mud. It had an open doorway and an open window directly across from the entrance. On the left wall, another aperture led to a smaller anteroom. The roof was a thick mass of intertwined sticks and twigs that rose in the middle about ten feet above the ground. From the heavy layer of dust on the dirt floor, I gathered that no one had been here for some time.

For a few moments I stood near the doorway to the smaller chamber. Then I sat down, hoping for a chance to sleep. Rafiq and Farzad did the same. A slight wind blew through the open door and window. It didn't take long for the heat from the hike to dissipate. This was going to be a cold night.

Hopeless and Ahmed left the shack and returned a few minutes later with armfuls of twigs and leaves. They laid these in the center of the room and quickly started an indoor campfire. From my spot just a few feet away, I caught the eyes of Hopeless and looked closely for a sign of compassion or empathy. There was none. I diverted my gaze to the fire.

When the heat grew too intense, I scooted back a few feet, pulled the hood of my jacket over my head, and leaned my head against the wall. It was almost comfortable. Despite the fact that I was a hostage, I was so exhausted I was sure I'd soon be snoozing.

Haqqani had other ideas, however. With quick gestures he emphatically waved me back toward the fire. The heat was scorching, but I did not want to upset my kidnappers, so I reluctantly rejoined the group. The three Taliban kept up a steady conversation among themselves. I stole a glance at Rafiq and Farzad for a clue to what was being said, but their tense expressions revealed little.

Then the tone of the conversation suddenly grew more strident. Haqqani looked at me and made slashing gestures across his throat. At this point no translation was necessary. They were discussing ways to end the lives of their hostages.

We sat in front of the fire for about an hour. Whenever the flames began to subside, Hopeless and Ahmed either went outside to gather more fuel or pulled off a few twigs from the roof to bring the fire back to life. Haqqani, meanwhile, produced a smartphone and listened to music from a radio station. Then he began flipping through different stations—some with music, others with conversation I couldn't understand.

All of a sudden Haqqani thrust his phone toward Rafiq, Farzad, and me. A video playing on the small screen depicted soldiers in camouflage NATO uniforms hitting and kicking Afghan men. This went on for several seconds. Then the video showed a man speaking in Arabic, which I later learned involved his commentary on the cruelty of NATO forces and the innocence of the people they killed.

There was more—Taliban leaders making speeches and recordings of multiple funerals for fallen Taliban fighters. In these scenes the camera showed women in black veils, wailing and bending over to kiss the face of a corpse in a casket. The most disturbing and gruesome clip portrayed an Afghan man, half dressed and half dead, who'd been tied up with a rope and attached to the back of a military truck. As the truck sped ahead, the man was dragged along behind it, his body jerking and bouncing in the dusty street.

Of course I felt compassion for the people depicted in these scenes. I was not so naïve as to believe that NATO forces were without fault or that they always treated their prisoners well. At the same time, I realized that these images were designed to manipulate emotions—in this case, ours. It felt like propaganda. Later I even wondered if some of the scenes might have been staged.

At the time, though, I felt Haqqani was signaling what was about to happen to us. It was a kind of psychological torture with the physical torture to follow.

Haqqani had a collection of these video clips on his phone, none longer than a minute in length. When we'd cycled through them all, they started again, playing in an endless loop. Judging by the dark intensity in Haqqani's eyes, it was clear there would be no rest on this night. We were expected to sit and watch as he held the phone up, the distressing images flickering a few inches from our faces.

This went on for an hour, then another. Ahmed eventually closed his eyes and fell asleep.

I desperately wanted the videos to stop. If Haqqani was trying to break us down emotionally, it was working, at least on me. I almost wished he'd move on to the physical torture just so I wouldn't have to endure the continuing displays of suffering and torment. More than once I tried to look away, but each time Haqqani's glare was enough to indicate this wasn't an option.

Finally, about three grueling hours after the videos started, Haqqani abruptly puts down the phone.

"You see how your people treat us?" he says to me through Rafiq's translation, anger in his voice. "We're not treating you this way, are we? We don't treat people like that."

"You guys have been good," I say. "Thank you. You've been treating me well."

My answer isn't enough to calm down Haqqani. Soon he launches into an animated speech as he stares at me. Rafiq tries to translate, but Haqqani doesn't wait for his words to be communicated. He keeps talking, almost shouting.

"Are you going to follow our demands? How quickly are you going to follow them?" are two phrases Rafiq is able to pass on. Then, a few minutes later, comes the threat that was never far from my mind: "We're going to kill you."

It seems to me that Haqqani is in tough-guy mode, that he is deliberately trying to intimidate and provoke me. And to some degree he is succeeding—certainly my thoughts and emotions are in turmoil. But

I don't want this Taliban leader to know it. I've already determined that I do not want to react to my kidnappers with fear or with hatred. I don't want to play their game. So I nod as Haqqani rants, but otherwise I say and show him nothing.

Even so, his words have left their mark. The yo-yo of my emotions have hit another trough.

It's no longer a matter of whether or not they're going to kill me. It's just a matter of how and when.

WHATEVER THIS IS

CHAPTER SEVEN

2:30 P.M., WEDNESDAY

COLORADO SPRINGS, COLORADO

DANIEL, MY BOSS, DRUMMED HIS FINGERS ON A TABLETOP. HE was uneasy. If I had known what he was facing, I would not have envied him.

He sat in a windowless room at the headquarters of Compassion International, where Cilicia worked. Joining him at the table were a Compassion vice president and chaplain, as well as Lars, Morning Star's executive director, and Anne, Daniel's wife.

I hate to do this, Daniel thought. *I hate for Cilicia to hear the news I'm going to bring her. But I have to do it.*

At about the same time another staff member at Compassion entered my wife's second-floor office and asked her to stop what she was doing and come with her. The woman escorted Cilicia to the room where everyone was waiting.

Daniel watched the alarm grow on Cilicia's face when she entered the room and absorbed who was present. *Lord, help me. I want this to be as clean and crisp as I can make it.*

"What are you doing here?" Cilicia asked, her eyes wide. Her coworker gently guided Cilicia to an open seat at the table.

Daniel took a deep breath. "Cilicia, I got a call from Kabul this morning. Dilip, Rafiq, and Farzad were supposed to be at dinner with Roy a few hours ago. They didn't call in and never showed up. Roy has been trying to reach them by phone for several hours and hasn't been able to make contact. We don't know where they are."

As Daniel and Lars had agreed before the meeting, Daniel made no mention of the visit and report from Rafiq's cousin. The last thing they wanted was to further distress Cilicia with what could turn out to be false information.

Cilicia kept her composure. "What does this really mean?" she asked. "What do we do?"

She is so strong, Daniel thought. "Does it mean that they're just out of cell phone range," he said, "or that they broke down somewhere, or that they've been kidnapped? We don't know yet. But I can tell you this. Number one, we want this contained. We don't want you to talk about this with anyone until we find out more. Number two, we'll give you information as soon as we get it. We want you to know that you and your family will get every bit of the support you need through this."

Daniel could see Cilicia's mind working through the scenarios and coming to the awful but most likely conclusion. Finally, the moment caught up with her. Her eyes filled with tears.

He didn't want to prolong her agony. "That's pretty much all we have right now," he said quietly. He stood, as did everyone else, and stepped around the table to give Cilicia a hug.

"We'll be here with you all the way through this," he whispered. "Whatever *this* is."

DEMANDS

CHAPTER EIGHT

5:45 A.M., THURSDAY, DECEMBER 6
MOUNTAIN RANGE EAST OF KABUL, AFGHANISTAN
THE FIRE INSIDE OUR SHACK WAS PETERING OUT. THE CUR-
rent leader of our Taliban captors ignored it. Haqqani was still bent
on intimidating us. He sat less than three feet away from me. Though
he didn't raise his voice, his eyes communicated an intensity that
demanded attention.

"Why are you here? What do you guys do? Where is your NGO
working?" Haqqani spit out the questions faster than Rafiq could
translate them. He didn't wait for our answers.

"Here are our demands."

Here it comes, I thought. We were finally about to learn the objective of our kidnapping.

The answer, not surprisingly, was money. Millions. I had trouble
understanding exactly how much, but it was clearly beyond any realistic possibility.

This wasn't good.

Then Rafiq said they were talking about a prisoner exchange—
the three of us for an unknown number of Taliban being held in the

notorious Pul-e-Charkhi prison east of Kabul. This also wasn't good. The prison, constructed in the 1970s, was infamous for the torture and executions of inmates after the 1978 Saur revolution and the war with the Soviets that followed. Though the United States had recently helped expand the prison and transferred people there from the detention facility in Guantanamo Bay, Cuba, living conditions for its two thousand or so inmates were still being criticized by human rights groups. The reputation of Pul-e-Charkhi had changed little over the years—those who went in rarely got out.

The mention of a second demand definitely troubled me. Why even bring up two demands? Was it possible that if someone somehow produced money for our release, we would still be sent to prison—or worse?

I didn't even want to think about that.

Haqqani continued his monologue, glaring at me as he explained that we would soon make a phone call to our NGO office. If we did not make quick progress toward meeting their demands, he said, the Taliban in Pakistan would come and take us. If we did not immediately follow his directions, they would execute us.

"You have three days to deliver the money," Haqqani said to me. For emphasis, he added another throat-slashing gesture.

My heart sank at this statement. I worked for a small nonprofit, with only five full-time employees in the United States. We simply did not have thousands of dollars, let alone millions, set aside for emergencies. My family was in the same situation.

Afghans who watch American movies and TV shows often have the impression that everyone in our country has servants and drives a sports car. Of course that isn't true. My family was certainly not wealthy. I didn't see how they could come up with funds that would even come close to satisfying our captors. And even if they did raise some money, this was Thursday. In Afghanistan, the weekend off-days are Thursday and Friday. Then starting Friday night, banks would begin closing for the weekend in the United States.

These men were not going to get any money in the next three days. There was no chance of satisfying their demands. None.

Perhaps it's a blessing that even in the midst of the most intense crisis, practical and routine matters will intervene to distract us. That was the case for me, when Haqqani finished with his demands and threats and left us to ponder the potentially dire consequences. As the first hints of dawn's light filtered through the shack's open doorway and window, I realized that I desperately needed to go to the bathroom.

I told Rafiq, who secured permission for me to leave the shack. I didn't know where I was and really had nowhere to go even if I wanted to attempt an escape, but I noticed that Hopeless had picked up his Kalashnikov and followed me out.

I shuddered in the crisp morning chill and looked around. There was no cover, nothing but dirt and air. *How am I going to find a little privacy?* I wondered. *Ah, what privacy? There's no such thing out here.*

I picked out a spot about fifty yards from the shack. The night before, I had seen Hopeless squat somewhere near there to urinate. I didn't want to offend my captors, so I tried to do the same. I have to admit, though, that between my long trousers and my unfamiliarity with the practice, I had more than a little trouble.

Despite the seriousness of my predicament, I had to stifle a chuckle. *If I do this wrong, I'm going to get shot while peeing. That would be the worst way to go!* At least it would be quick. I'd already made up my mind that I preferred to face death straight on, with no delay, rather than endure a lengthy torture.

When I returned to the shack, I learned that it was time to walk again. Soon we were back on the trail, moving deeper into the mountains on the crisp, hazy morning. Was this going to be another marathon hike? I hoped not. But I had greater concerns than the nagging ache in my legs.

As we again followed the rises and dips of a trail that only my captors understood, I found the silence unnerving. Since they were supposedly moving closer to achieving their goal, I expected them to clarify plans among themselves, perhaps even to show a smile or two. But there was no interaction at all, just a grim stillness.

I couldn't erase the threatening images of both Haqqani and Ahmed looking at me and cutting a hand across their throats. They seemed almost eager to put an end to me. On the other hand, they'd already had ample time and opportunity to kill me, and I was still here. Would this be my last day on earth? I had no answer. There was nothing else to do but keep walking and hoping.

About an hour after we'd started up again, what looked like a two-story, mud-walled building appeared on the horizon. Smoke rose from the chimney. It was easily the largest structure I'd seen since the abduction. As we got closer, I noticed it had no windows. I wondered if it was a warehouse though I couldn't imagine what might be stored there. Next to it I saw a cement rectangle about fifteen feet wide and thirty-five feet long, its walls three feet high. Inside it was a pool of water.

We did not stop there, however. As we passed, I tried to memorize the scene in case I had the chance to describe it later. Any landmark in this desolate territory was rare indeed.

We turned a corner on the trail. About fifty yards to our left was what looked like a home, or at least a sturdy shelter. To my surprise, we turned off our path and walked toward it.

We were about halfway there when our view opened up to a flat, barren valley. More than a hundred yards ahead were three more structures. The largest of these was about fifty feet long and closed up—I saw no doorway or windows. The other two had clearly been abandoned for some time. Neither had a roof, and the crumbling walls of one appeared to top out at about four feet high.

We approached the shelter on our left. This house of stone, brick, and mud had three rooms, though only the largest of the rooms had a roof over it. I stooped as we entered this room through the low, open doorway, which was the only entrance or exit. The space was about twenty by twenty-five feet and, unlike our previous stop, had been used recently. Several mats and blankets lay scattered on the dirt floor. To our left in an indent in the wall was a fire pit. A kettle with burn marks sat on a pair of stones next to a pile of blackened wood. A few embers still glowed.

Near the middle of the room, a single wood pole stretched to the ceiling to support the thatched roof. There were two openings in the wall for ventilation, too small to be called windows. In the far corner a shelf had been built into the wall. On the shelf were a candle, a notebook, and an item wrapped in silk. I later learned this was a Koran.

The room appeared to me to be a well-maintained space for meetings or guests. I eventually found out that despite its modest exterior, Rafiq and Farzad had immediately recognized this place as something else: a mosque. Though they said nothing, they were irate. Both had a similar thought: *How can these people call themselves Muslims and hold us as prisoners in a holy place?*

Our captors quickly began constructing a new fire and preparing for a round of green tea. Suddenly a young man wearing a black-and-white-checkered headscarf and carrying a plastic tub of sugar walked through the doorway. The Taliban paid little attention to this supply man. I gave him a smile, hoping to make some kind of connection, but he turned away, apparently indifferent, before leaving the room.

I took little comfort in the improvement in our surroundings. It appeared this was all part of a well-planned operation. I had the definite impression that these guys had done this before.

We were in the middle of our tea when a fourth Talib entered the room. I recognized him as one of our original abductors, one of the two younger ones. He wore a gray vest over his *salwar kameez*. His face and slightly wavy brown hair were caked in dust. He had a short, uneven beard. His teeth were crooked; part of a front tooth was missing.

What I noticed most about him was that he seemed a natural leader—and that he immediately made a point of looking intently at me and smiling.

The new arrival entered into an animated conversation with the other three Taliban. From their gestures, facial expressions, and use of the word *Wallakah*—the same word that had been repeatedly shouted the night before—I decided that this was the new guy's name and that they were discussing his failure to show up. It wasn't an argument. I sensed that the others accepted his explanation.

There was something different about Wallakah. He was quite engaging and did most of the talking. He also continued to glance my way to make eye contact. For some reason it didn't feel threatening.

Sometimes he even smiled and put his hand over his heart as if to say, "It's going to be all right."

After more discussion between Wallakah and the older captors, we all sat down to finish our tea. One of the Taliban produced naan that had been left over from the previous night. This seemed to be a welcome sight, not only to Rafiq, Farzad, and me but also to our abductors. I knew I was hungry. Although the bread was now hard, it was almost tasty, especially after dipping it in the hot tea.

Once tea was over, Wallakah waved the rest of us toward the door. Rafiq explained: "We're going to make that phone call."

I tried to swallow the apprehension that rose like bile in my throat. *If they ask me to talk, what will I say? I need to choose my words carefully. I want to share as much as I can, but I don't want to say anything that will upset these guys.* Then I remembered that none of our captors spoke English. Other than words that were common to our multiple languages, they wouldn't understand anything I said.

All of us but Ahmed walked toward a neighboring mountain, where I suspected the cell reception was better. I felt tense but had also noticed a change in the atmosphere since Wallakah's arrival. Haqqani had given up his threats and gestures, at least for now. Clearly a new man was in charge.

It took only a minute to reach the base of the hill. The Taliban called this place Black Mountain, no doubt because it was covered with bushes as tall as a man, each filled with greenish-black, almond-shaped nuts. As we neared the top, Rafiq whispered to me, "When we get connected, say everything. I will keep these guys occupied."

Obviously Rafiq was still thinking strategically. It was a measure of comfort. Though I certainly wouldn't wish this experience on anyone, I was so glad I had my two friends with me.

When we reached a plateau, Wallakah turned to me. There were no smiles now. It was time for business.

He handed a cell phone to me and another to Rafiq. "We want the phone number to your colleagues in Kabul," Wallakah said.

I had Roy's number on a sheet of paper that I usually carried in my backpack. Anticipating this request, I'd removed the paper just before we left the mosque and put it in my pocket. Before I could take it out, however, Rafiq started paging through the contact list on the phone he'd been given until he found Roy's number. They had apparently inserted our SIM cards into their phones. I checked the contact list in the phone in my hand. Sure enough, I recognized the names.

Wallakah addressed me via Rafiq's translation: "Talk to them. Tell them we want twenty million dollars. Or we turn you over to Pakistan Taliban. Or we kill you."

"Wait. What do you mean, 'twenty million dollars'?" I asked.

Haqqani jumped in with a correction. "No, it's two million dollars." They talked for a few moments as if trying to make up their minds.

This didn't make any sense. My frustration made me bold. "Look, if you guys want me to negotiate for our release," I said, "you have to agree on a dollar amount."

It was insane, really. I was telling *them* how to conduct a hostage negotiation. But after further back and forth, I figured out that part of the problem was they were talking in Pakistani rupees while I was thinking U.S. dollars.

The other part of the problem was that they hadn't yet decided how much they were asking. Maybe they weren't as experienced as I thought.

Once we got the issue of currency straightened out, they bounced between a demand ranging from three hundred thousand to five hundred thousand U.S. dollars. I got them to settle on the three hundred thousand figure—at least that's what I thought we agreed on. Not that it mattered much. It might as well have been three hundred million. No one I knew had that kind of money.

Wallakah finally gestured to the phone in my hand. "Okay," he said, "make the call."

At that point I could have called anyone in the world—I didn't think these guys would know the difference. I briefly considered calling Cilicia or someone else in my family, but what would I say? Although I realized Morning Star would be wondering what had happened to me, I assumed no one yet knew we'd been kidnapped. How could I call Cilicia and say, "I've been abducted. I don't know if I'm going to survive this"? I didn't want to give her that burden.

I also didn't know if I could handle the conversation emotionally. What if I broke down when I heard Cilicia's voice and couldn't speak? That wouldn't help either one of us.

I decided it was better to call Roy and let my colleagues know what was happening. They would know what to do.

I punched the preset number for Roy and waited.

"Hello?"

"Roy, it's Dilip. I hope you have an idea of what happened to us." My words came out fast but mostly steady.

"Yes, Dilip, we have an idea."

"Well, let me explain a bit more so you have a better understanding of what's been happening." I related some of the details of how we'd been abducted, that we were being fed, and that for now we were all right.

"Are they treating you okay?" Roy asked. "Have they given any indication they're about to harm you?"

"No, not yet," I said. "Other than threats and gestures of throat-cutting."

Then I relayed our kidnappers' demands—as well as the three-day timeline.

It was about this time that the phone in Rafiq's hand rang. When I heard the sound of a woman crying, I realized that the caller was his wife. While I continued to talk with Roy, I watched Wallakah take Rafiq's phone and start to talk. He seemed to be reassuring her that everything was going to be fine.

A few minutes later Rafiq's phone rang again. This time it was Farzad's son. Though Farzad kept his own voice calm, I could hear the distress and desperation in the voice on the other end of the call. They spoke for less than a minute.

Now that phones with our SIM cards were in service, family members who'd been frantically calling without success were finally getting through. Though I tried to stay focused on my conversation with Roy, it was heartbreaking to hear Rafiq and Farzad describe our plight amid the tears and strained voices of their loved ones. I thought again about calling Cilicia. Once again, I decided it was better if I didn't.

"Dilip, do you know which direction you traveled during that long hike: east, west, north, south?" Roy asked.

I had to admit I had no idea.

At one point I handed the phone to Rafiq. He got right to the point. "This is really serious, Roy," he said. "They are demanding this. Our lives are at risk. We need the dollars transferred now."

Rafiq handed the phone back to me.

"Dilip, I need to tell you that this process is probably not going to happen on the timetable they want," Roy said in a calm voice. "These things tend to move slowly. I know that's not what you want to hear, brother. But it's better for you if it's not rushed."

"I know," I said. "But these guys *are* serious. If we don't respond quickly, they might harm us."

"Well, believe me, we are going to be doing everything we possibly can to bring you guys back safely," Roy said. We all agreed that we would make another phone call at five that evening and then said our good-byes.

We'd done it. We had made contact with the outside world. To my surprise, we'd been allowed to talk with Roy for about twenty minutes.

I was reassured by the sincerity and steadiness in Roy's voice. I knew that my colleagues, friends, and family would indeed make every effort to secure our safe release. I still didn't know what fate awaited me, but just having that connection with a coworker and friend had left me feeling encouraged.

On the walk back down Black Mountain, I noticed a couple pieces of brown cloth half buried in the dirt. Without breaking stride, I bent down, scooped them up, and put them in my jacket pocket. No one seemed to notice. Part of me wanted to save them as a souvenir. The other part thought that if necessary, they would come in handy as a substitute for toilet paper.

I was becoming more optimistic again and, perhaps, more resourceful. In other words, I was learning how to survive as a hostage.

THE CONVERSATION

CHAPTER NINE

10:00 A.M., THURSDAY

LIFE AS A PRISONER OF THE TALIBAN COULD BE A BIT SUR-real. On this day it certainly felt that way to me.

We were back in the thatch-roofed room of brick, stone, and mud that Rafiq and Farzad recognized as a mosque. While we three hostages leaned against the wall and tried to get some desperately needed rest, the four Taliban sat in a circle and talked among themselves.

"What are they saying?" I whispered to Rafiq.

"Nothing to do with us," he whispered back. "It's all local things—religion and politics."

Religion and politics. Most of the Afghans I knew—in fact, most people I knew, no matter where they were from—loved to express their opinions on these two time-honored topics. Apparently what was true for the rest of the world was also true among the Taliban. I watched as they shared their thoughts, sometimes smiling or laughing, other times with earnest expressions.

Islam was by far the predominant religion in Afghanistan. Roughly 80 percent of the people belonged to the Sunni denomination, including the Taliban, while as much as 19 percent were members of the

Shia branch of Islam.[1] The Taliban represented only a small segment of the Sunni population. (One recent estimate placed the number of rebel fighters at twenty-five thousand.[2]) That segment practiced a particularly extreme version of the Sunni religion, one that rejected any compromise with moderate Islam or traditional values.

In recent history Afghan Muslims had been largely tolerant of each other's religious differences. That began to change, however, during the bloody civil war in the 1990s. The conflict pitted sects and ethnic groups against one another. When the Taliban gained military and political power, anyone who disagreed with them suffered. The Hazara, Persian-speaking Shiites living primarily in central Afghanistan, were victims of multiple massacres. Author and journalist Ahmed Rashid wrote, "While the Taliban claim they are fighting a jihad against corrupt, evil Muslims, the ethnic minorities see them as using Islam as a cover to exterminate non-Pashtuns."[3]

I wondered what our captors were saying. Were they discussing a recent confrontation or battle? Were they expressing their admiration for the Taliban way of life? How could they defend a society that so easily embraced intimidation, terrorism, and murder? It was strange to watch this casual conversation while we sat just a few feet away, not knowing if or when they might decide to end our lives as well.

It must have been about eleven that morning when the supply guy returned to our room carrying fresh naan and another dish in a steel bowl. It was time for lunch.

Rafiq, Farzad, and I sat cross-legged in a circle with our captors. The main course was freshly cooked potato curry. It looked like something I would make for our family in our kitchen at home. Both the naan and the curry were passed around then placed on top of a mat in the middle of the circle where anyone could reach them for seconds.

After several minutes of eating and small talk by the Taliban, I began to feel full. Wallakah looked at me and said, "Did you get enough? Please eat more." To be polite, I took another helping of curry.

As we ate, I thought about the importance of food and mealtimes in the communal life of cultures. There was something about the shared experience of replenishing ourselves with tea, naan, stew, or curry that broke down barriers and encouraged relaxed and heartfelt communication. It was a practice as old as history. Sitting and eating here in the same manner as people had centuries before, I felt a connection to them I couldn't fully explain.

I also recalled Haqqani's comment from earlier that morning: "We're not treating you this way, are we? We don't treat people like that." It was true that we weren't being mistreated. We were given regular square meals and, in fact, were invited to share in everything that the Taliban ate. There was no sense of hoarding or possessiveness. It was in some ways a contrast to Western materialism.

I found myself caught between feelings of revulsion and admiration for my captors.

When Wallakah again implored me to eat more, I raised my hands to indicate I was more than satisfied. "Thank you," I said, as I nodded to each of the Taliban in turn, "for the wonderful lunch."

With a full stomach and after the long hike of the previous night and the events of the morning, I felt exhaustion overtaking me. I sensed no immediate threat. I retreated to a spot against the wall as did Rafiq and Farzad to my right. Haqqani moved to sit next to Farzad. To their right was the fire pit.

I leaned my head against the wall. I was ready for a nap.

Wallakah, however, had something else in mind. He sat back against the pole near the center of the room, about five feet away from me. He looked at me and said through Rafiq's translation, "Could I ask you some questions?"

I'd begun to establish a bit of rapport with Wallakah. Exhausted as I was, I certainly didn't want to jeopardize that now. I sat back up.

"Sure," I said. "Absolutely. I will try to answer any questions that you have."

"Where did you meet your wife?"

I studied Wallakah's face. I saw only curiosity there, but I remained guarded. After all, this still could be the man who would pull the trigger to end my life.

"We met in college," I said.

"Did you fall in love with her from the beginning, or was it a gradual progression?"

"I fell in love right away," I answered, "but our love has progressed and deepened since then."

Wallakah didn't hesitate. As soon as Rafiq finished his translation of my answer, my captor launched into his next question.

"Do you still love her?"

"We have our differences, of course. But I love her today more than ever. She is the only woman I have ever loved."

The questions kept coming, about my four children, about my father and mother and their occupations, about my in-laws, my aunties and uncles and their children, and all their careers. I wondered, *Is he trying to get a feel for my family's overall financial clout? Is the purpose of this to help him establish an appropriate ransom?*

I again examined Wallakah's posture and facial expressions. He was leaning forward, apparently eager to hear every word. There was a kind of glee in his eyes. I didn't sense that our conversation was about money. It felt more like intense curiosity. I decided that he was simply taking advantage of the incredibly rare opportunity to talk with and learn more about an outsider, someone different from him.

As the questions continued, I stole glances at the others in the room. Rafiq and Farzad both seemed to be listening intently. Haqqani was actually smiling, apparently enjoying our conversation. It was nothing like his earlier demeanor.

Ahmed sat behind Wallakah and to his left. His expression was neutral; I couldn't tell if he cared about our conversation or not. To Wallakah's left, almost against the far wall, was Hopeless. For an instant my eyes caught his, and I realized he could not have been more indifferent. He was always fiddling with something—his shoes or his prayer beads. This time it was his Kalashnikov, and it was pointed at me. I found myself praying that the gun would not go off while he cleaned it. I would rather be taken out in the wild and shot intentionally than be killed by a misfire while talking casually in this shelter.

"Where do your cousins work?" Wallakah asked me. "Why do they live there?" I tried to explain my extended family's whereabouts and motivations. Wallakah's questions were more evidence to me that the Taliban, like other Afghans, defined themselves first by their families, which included their extended families, and their people group.

"Which of your cousins are you closest to?" Wallakah asked.

"I'm naturally closest to those who live near and that I see most often," I said. "But we try to all get together at least once or twice a year."

As I answered this question, I noticed Ahmed tearing up. I didn't understand why but didn't want to interrupt the conversation with

Wallakah to ask. For all I knew, it was just dust bothering his eyes. Later, however, Rafiq told me that Ahmed had been complaining to the other insurgents. "I didn't want to be part of a kidnapping," Ahmed told them. "I thought we were going to recover money that was owed to you. You lied to me." Apparently my sharing about my family triggered more regret and a tearful reaction.

It was shortly after I observed this change in Ahmed that Hopeless gave me a dark look, then spat out a few words in the direction of Wallakah and Haqqani. They ignored him.

To my surprise, Farzad then put his finger to his lips and briefly spoke to Hopeless in a calm, even dignified manner. Whatever he said, Hopeless took it without comment or retaliation.

Months later I learned what was actually said during this exchange.

Hopeless: "Why are you talking to this donkey's son? Just give me the word and I'll end it all."

Farzad: "Shh. We are not going to be talking about such things."

When I found out what Hopeless had said, I was glad Rafiq chose not to translate at the time.

A few minutes after Hopeless expressed his desire to put an end to the "donkey's son," Haqqani provided the explanation for Hopeless's attitude. He gestured at Hopeless and said, "He has a mission. He's been assigned to take your truck and perform a suicide bombing in Kabul next week."

No wonder Hopeless looked so hopeless! His anger and emotional distance now made perfect sense.

I'd heard stories that in some madrassas, students were taught that a glorious eternity was in store for them if they gave their lives to kill "infidels." Paradise was a place where blue skies and virgin girls awaited suicide attackers.

Based on the behavior of Hopeless, however, I didn't think he truly believed it. He and others like him tried to act in a way they thought would please God, yet they had no joy or hope over it. It seemed they had only uncertainty in their minds and spirits.

I actually felt sorry for him.

Wallakah still paid no attention to Hopeless and continued his questioning. After more than an hour of queries about my family, our conversation took an abrupt and more personal turn.

"If I put a gun in your hand, would you find it easy to kill someone?" he asked.

I was startled by the question, but my answer was blunt. "No," I said, shaking my head. "I could not bring myself to hurt someone that way. I am trained as a doctor to save people's lives. Even if I was not a doctor, my faith and personality would not allow me to do this."

It was Wallakah's turn to be blunt. "I have killed many people," he said. "This is all I've done in my life—kill people." I noticed that there was no pride in his words. Then this apparently ruthless murderer surprised me with the depth of his thinking. He compared and analyzed our lives.

"You do these humanitarian projects because of what your father and your family taught you when you were growing up," he said. "The reason I do what I do is because it is what my father showed me. He taught me everything that I know. This is all I watched my father do until I was five years old—kill people. Then he was arrested, and I joined the Taliban. My father is thirty-four years old and has been in Pul-e-Charkhi prison in Kabul for the last fourteen years."

Sadness washed over Wallakah's face when he spoke about his father. After his words were translated, I interjected a comment of my own.

"You are nineteen years old," I said. "I am thirty-nine years old. I am old enough to be your father."

This brought a grin back to Wallakah's face.

"I am a father myself," he said. "I have a one-year-old son." I noticed he did not add that he wanted his son to follow in his father's footsteps.

I was astonished. Through our conversation, I had connected with this young man, a teenager who looked so much older, a teenager who had personally and violently taken many lives. Despite our divergent backgrounds and my horror at the atrocities he had committed, I could converse with him based on the common threads that linked us as husbands, fathers, and sons . . . as human beings.

During past visits to Afghanistan, I'd wondered more than once what I would say if I ever had the chance to speak with an active member of the Taliban. Given what I knew of their hatred of foreigners, particularly Americans, I expected it would be nearly impossible to get them to even listen to me, let alone convince them that they had other options for the future and how to view life. I now realized that my own views would also have been an obstacle to any meaningful interaction. I hated how they intimidated their fellow Afghans in rural areas, and I deplored the violence they perpetrated against anyone they perceived as an enemy. I had categorized them as inhumane, wild cannibals who wanted nothing to do with a civilized way of life and would do anything to preserve their way of living and thinking.

Now, in the midst of my heart-to-heart talk with Wallakah, I realized that the picture might be a bit more complicated.

The surprises on this day were not over. Wallakah began asking me detailed questions about life in the United States. Since the Taliban were famous for seeing America as the "Great Satan," I did not expect this. But perhaps I should not have been surprised. When I met people on my travels around the world, everyone had an opinion about the United States, either positive or critical. Yet people were also always curious. Wallakah, it seemed, was no exception.

After I had answered a few of his questions about the United States, Wallakah stunned me once again: "Could you take me to America?"

I blinked and tried to hide my shock. The idea was outlandish, but I didn't want to discourage him.

"Yes, that is possible," I said. "The U.S. has its problems, but it is still the greatest place to live on earth simply because of the fact that you can exercise freedom and liberty as an individual. When people use that freedom and liberty for the overall good of their society, it has an overwhelmingly positive impact on the individual and on society."

Wallakah shifted his position and leaned even closer to me. I saw the excitement in his eyes.

"What steps would I take to start the process?" he asked.

"You would first need to go to Kabul and apply for a passport and visa." I tried to imagine a member of the Taliban going to the U.S. Embassy and filling out papers to enter the United States.

"I have never been out of the country," he said. "I've never even been to Kabul. What would I do if I came to America? Could I start my life over again? Could I further my education there?"

"Yes, there are many educational opportunities," I said. "You could train for a new career and make a new start."

Wallakah's grin grew even larger. I could almost see the wheels turning in his mind. I wondered if he'd ever had the opportunity to sit down with someone and talk about other options for his life.

I was amazed. It was as if Wallakah was saying openly what all of these insurgents must have sensed in their hearts, though they wouldn't admit it—that there was something more to life than what they were currently pursuing and experiencing.

I was struck by the irony of our circumstances. These men had their guns pointed at me and had complete control of the situation, yet they were operating under a heavy blanket of fear. They feared change—they wanted to hold tightly to the only way of life they knew. They feared the outsiders that they believed came to pollute and dilute their society and its rich culture and traditions. They feared a god that they believed waited to punish them the moment they stepped out of line.

At the same time, I was the one sitting and staring at the barrels of loaded Kalashnikovs, the one knowing that my life could end at any moment. Yet I was also the one who lived with hope. I had gained hope from trying to bring blessings to others out of the blessings I'd received. I had hope from teaching Afghans about basic health education and seeing how that bettered their lives. I had hope that sprang from getting out of my comfort zone and following my dream of meeting the needs of the downtrodden and forgotten. I had hope in even the worst circumstances because I believed in a God who loved me unconditionally.

Yet in his fear one of these terrorists also dared to hope—for a chance to start over, a chance to become more than a killing machine.

And perhaps he was not alone, for Haqqani now entered the conversation. "Would you keep in touch with us," he asked, "after you are released and you rejoin your family in the U.S.?"

He was talking about my release? This was a good sign!

"I would love to keep in touch with both of you," I said, nodding to Wallakah and Haqqani. I wanted to reciprocate further, so I picked up my notebook and started to write down my cell phone number. It was almost as if we were at a coffee shop back home, exchanging business cards. I half-expected these two to pull out a piece of paper and write down their own contact information, though in the next instant I remembered that they were constantly changing phones and SIM cards to avoid being tracked. Of course they didn't have a regular phone number. Then I wondered if my own number would be passed into the hands of other insurgents and further complicate my chances for release. I stopped writing.

Wallakah was still smiling. "I would very much like to keep in contact with you," he said. Haqqani voiced his agreement.

We had been talking for nearly three hours. Wallakah finally and graciously drew our conversation to a close: "Thank you so much for being very open in answering all my questions. You did not deter from any of them and answered all of them with much patience and kindness. I want to thank you so much for doing this."

I also expressed my thanks and then leaned back against the wall of the shelter, feeling a new wave of exhaustion cascading over me. Despite my fatigue, I was flooded with thoughts. How easy it was to live with assumptions, prejudice, and hatred toward others and cut off any chance for relationship. To move forward required effort, commitment, a thirst for human connection. It demanded respect and even love for one another.

In Wallakah, a man most people would regard as a terrorist, I had seen respect and a thirst for connection. Earlier in the day I wondered how, or if, I would ever relate to my kidnappers so that they saw me not as an enemy or resource to trade for cash but as a fellow human being. Yet it was one of them who initiated the link. All we had to do was talk about the basic things that all people relate to: family, relationships, aspirations, love, hope. It was enough to cut through our differences in culture and worldview.

I wondered what impression I'd left on these stalwarts of mujahideen and Taliban tradition. Nearly everything they knew of Western civilization probably came from movies and the media and led them to categorize all foreigners as infidels. I hoped our interaction would lead them to rethink their ideology.

Moments later I had surprising and satisfying evidence that my words and actions had made an impression. Wallakah and Haqqani had continued to talk. I had no idea what they were saying, of course, but Rafiq had been listening. Now my friend leaned toward me and whispered, "Wallakah just said, 'This guy is our captive, and yet he seems so much at peace. He is a better Muslim than we are.'"

I could hardly believe my ears.

I'd wondered how my kidnappers might be "reading" me. Now I had an inkling that they had indeed observed something different about me and were at least thinking about what that meant.

My captors were not the only ones who were rethinking long-held views. Our conversation had also caused me to reevaluate my perspective. How could I pass judgment on Wallakah for how he'd turned out? He had experienced nothing but chaos and conflict his entire life. From the beginning, killing was modeled as a lifestyle. I thought of my father, who had shown me a different way to live by dedicating his life to helping others. In my mind I commended Wallakah's willingness to open his eyes. Even as he sensed the futility of his current existence, he grasped at something more.

As I drifted off to sleep, my spirit remained excited by Wallakah's curiosity and dreams.

I may die soon, even today, but if so I think I will die satisfied. My job here is done. I have connected with a member of the Taliban and given us both much to think about—that no matter our circumstances we still have choices in life, that despite our perceived differences we both are human beings with much more in common than we realize.

CONNECTIONS

CHAPTER TEN

3:45 P.M., THURSDAY

THE ATMOSPHERE IN OUR LITTLE CAMP HAD CERTAINLY changed after the long conversation with Wallakah. When I woke from a thirty-minute nap—not nearly enough sleep to counter the exhaustion that was overtaking me—our captors seemed almost cheerful.

It was time for another round of tea. Nothing better represented the culture and tradition of Afghanistan than the sharing of green tea. As I had already learned during my previous visits to the country, the purpose of serving tea was about more than a break or quick refreshment. It was a social event.

Tea leaves from Pakistan were driven daily into Afghanistan by the truckload. When someone decided it was time for tea, which generally happened several times a day, a handful of tea plants and leaves were thrown into a kettle of steaming water. Before the leaves were fully soaked, someone poured some of this mild tea into a glass (cups were rarely seen in Afghanistan's rural areas). This wasn't for drinking. Instead, this same hot water was poured from one glass to another to "wash" all the glasses. When this process was complete and the tea was ready, the host served everyone. More often than not, each serving included a generous portion of sugar. Afghans seemed to like a lot of sugar in their tea—a fifth of a glass or more.

It was rare for anyone to stop after just one serving. The focus was not on the tea but on the conversation it stimulated. Chores and other responsibilities seemed to be forgotten as those present shared what was on their minds and spent time developing relationships. This could easily go on for more than an hour.

Our Taliban "hosts" were no exception to this custom. Once we'd all gathered in a circle and had filled glasses in hand, the conversation flowed. When even Hopeless joined in the animated discussion, I wondered what topic could have attracted his interest.

Rafiq filled me in—they were discussing our abduction and analyzing how well they'd performed. Then Haqqani asked Rafiq, "What did you think of the capture? We accomplished it quickly, yes?"

"Yes, it happened very quickly," Rafiq said. "As the driver, I had very little time to react. You did well."

All four Taliban seemed pleased with this comment. A few of them chuckled. Even Rafiq and Farzad laughed.

I didn't laugh. I was irritated that our captors were kidnapping people, then talking about their techniques as if they were analyzing their swings on the tennis court. I was even a bit miffed that Rafiq and Farzad were encouraging them. I was glad no one asked me for my opinion of the abduction.

At the same time, I understood and admired what Rafiq, in particular, was doing. During the last two days, he had consistently engaged our captors in conversation, asking simple questions and sometimes offering compliments. It helped reduce the tension and created more of a team environment instead of "us versus them."

Then our captors began asking me questions, but they had nothing to do with abductions. Instead, the topic was Indian movies. I suppose it was natural, given my background and the historically positive relationship between Afghanistan and India, but even so it surprised me.

"Have you seen any actors—Dilip Kumar, Amitabh Bachchan, Shahrukh Khan, Amir Khan, Salman Khan, Saif Ali Khan?" Haqqani asked.

I shook my head and explained I'd seen only a few South Indian movie stars, ones they were unlikely to know.

I thought they might also talk about Hollywood stars, but the focus remained on Indian actors. Afghans have long enjoyed the cinematic efforts of their neighbors in India. Even after the Taliban takeover, copies of these movies continued to make their way into the country via the black market. I found it ironic that I was discussing movies with these guys even though the Taliban considered them illegal.

"You're a handsome guy—you should be acting in movies yourself," Wallakah said.

"Thank you," I replied. I appreciated the compliment but couldn't help feeling strange about it.

We certainly were developing a sense of camaraderie. The conversation felt like many others I'd had over tea with villagers during previous trips. The only difference at this moment was the sight of Hopeless, who continued to frown under his long beard and clean his Kalashnikov as we talked. At least I now understood why he was so morose.

A few minutes later Wallakah and Haqqani picked up their weapons and gestured for us to leave the shelter. I wondered where we were going. It couldn't have been time for our five o'clock call to Roy yet.

Early or not, we did hike up Black Mountain. Once again Wallakah pulled out a cell phone. Instead of handing it to me, however, he stared at its screen for a few moments.

"It looks like they cut off the signal early today," he said. I didn't understand exactly how, but apparently the Taliban controlled cell reception in this area. "There's nothing now. Let's try again tomorrow."

As Rafiq translated, Wallakah turned and began walking down the mountain. An expressionless Haqqani prodded us to follow. Just like that, our phone attempt was over.

I was a bit stunned by the Taliban's response. Our captors wanted their money in three days. Now because of a technical difficulty, they'd lost a chance to move things forward. Yet they didn't seem angry or frustrated at all.

I realized I was looking at the situation from my Western perspective. It had been two days since I'd checked my e-mail. I'd been cut off from the gadgets I was so used to: smartphones, computers, iPods, iPads, i-anythings. Now our cell reception had been cut off. I was upset that a technology failure had prevented me from connecting with my lifeline to the outside world. I expected them to be upset also.

But these guys lived a simple life. They weren't as tied in to gadgets and schedules. They were more flexible than a gymnast—if something didn't work out the way they wanted, they accepted it and were able to move on without handwringing or drama.

Though I was disappointed by the failed phone call, in another sense I was relieved. If we had to wait for tomorrow to continue negotiations, I was likely to live at least another day.

Not surprisingly, following another tea session back at the shelter, I needed to relieve myself. After I secured permission, Ahmed escorted me past the large house with the pool that we'd seen when we first arrived and toward the two roofless, abandoned shacks. His AK-47, slung by its strap on his shoulder, bounced against his side as we walked.

Ahmed pointed at one of the crumbling shacks; then he went to lean against the long building that sat near the two shacks, a spot where he could still see me.

I stepped "inside" the rubble of the shack he'd pointed out. Its walls were too low to hide my head. For a moment I considered my options. *Do I have a chance to escape here?*

Then I recalled a comment Haqqani had made to us that morning: "I'm glad you guys didn't try to escape during our walk yesterday. If you had rolled down the hill or tried to run, we would have shot and killed you."

No, I decided. My chances of getting away in these desolate mountains from four guys who knew the terrain and had guns were practically zero.

Once I'd urinated, I sat down behind the wall for some privacy and to think. After the scary and shocking events of the last two days, it was a relief to have even a moment alone. The same questions that had formed at the time of our abduction continued to tumble through my mind. Would Rafiq, Farzad, and I survive this and see our families again? If not, how and when would we die?

I remembered a statement Roy had made on the phone that morning: "Dilip, I want you to remember this. If there's a rescue effort, I want you guys to lie down and put your hands where people can clearly see them."

I continued to hope that we'd get out of this mess, but a rescue effort—especially a successful one—seemed highly unlikely to me. We were continually surrounded by experienced men with guns. Despite the connections I'd made with these guys, the fact remained that they were Taliban and we were their hostages. If a rescue attempt really was launched, a quick death seemed the far more likely outcome than liberation.

Back at the shelter I noticed someone had left a jug of water out for me in the entryway before the doorway. It felt good to wash my hands and face for the first time since our capture. It was a normal thing to do at a time when normal seemed rarer than a four-leaf clover.

Inside, I sat next to Rafiq against the wall. Our captors talked among themselves for about five minutes. Then Haqqani, sitting on the other side of Rafiq, spoke to him in a polite tone while looking at me.

"He would like to know," Rafiq said, "if you would give permission for him to ask you for medical advice."

This was indeed a rare request. "Yes, of course," I said.

"Can you tell me," Haqqani said, "what is wrong with my arm?"

I'd already noticed that Haqqani held his arm out stiffly and often flexed the fingers on his left hand. I moved to sit next to him. I massaged his fingers, feeling for abnormalities, and then had him move each finger in different directions.

Haqqani explained that he'd lost his sense of feeling in two of the fingers.

"When did this start?" I asked.

"It was after I was shot in a gunfight with the Afghan police and army," he said matter-of-factly. "They had been tracking our movements. The bullet is still inside me." He pulled his shirt down so that I could see the scar where the bullet had entered his chest.

"We made it out," he added, a tinge of pride in his voice. "We were fighting for the right cause. It was worth it."

I wasn't going to debate him on the validity of his actions. Instead, realizing he probably had nerve paralysis, I suggested some finger exercises and massages that might moderately improve his condition and sensation. If things didn't improve, I said, I recommended surgery to correct the nerve damage.

I realized as soon as I said it that surgery was unlikely. The Taliban were constantly on the move. They also distrusted doctors, hospitals, and Western medicine. It was amazing that Haqqani was allowing me, a foreigner, to examine him at all.

I'd been holding Haqqani's hand while examining his fingers and continued to do so while suggesting treatments. It occurred to me that in light of this man's lifestyle, he rarely, if ever, had the chance to be touched, held, cared for, or listened to.

A second and more chilling thought followed. *Wait a second. Osama bin Laden had a personal doctor. What if they decide they like me so much that they never release me and continue to use me for their benefit?*

Haqqani may have sensed the conflicting ideas running through my brain. He suddenly withdrew his hand. The look on his face was something close to embarrassment.

The "exam" was over.

"I appreciate you giving me this advice," he said. It had been a satisfying exchange. I'd made a deeper connection with the same man who'd been threatening me with execution that very morning.

The feeling of momentum and comradeship was so strong that I decided to take a chance. I looked at Hopeless and said, "How are you?"

He didn't snarl or shoot me. Instead, he nodded at me and put his hand over his heart as if to say, "I'm fine." Clearly he wasn't ready to be chums with his captives. Even so, it was the closest we'd come to a friendly interaction.

Ahmed, who'd been watching all this, now got up and sat beside me. He spoke to me in an animated voice. Rafiq translated most of what Ahmed was saying, but there was an English word neither Rafiq nor I could get.

I should have tried harder to understand because with one sudden move Ahmed had his arms locked around my head.

What? Help!

The brief panic I felt quickly subsided, however, when I heard laughter. I realized the word Ahmed had been saying was *wrestling*. He'd been trying to ask if I liked wrestling!

As soon as I escaped the headlock, I explained that I didn't enjoy that sport. *Besides,* I thought, *I was way too old to be wrestling with a strong young man like this guy.*

Ahmed said he loved wrestling. He puffed out his chest to demonstrate his strength. At this, the rest of the Taliban laughed again. I nodded and smiled, showing I agreed that Ahmed was certainly strong.

Our dinner was freshly heated naan and a spinach dish. It reminded me of a spinach dinner that Cilicia made often. But this one was bland. Cilicia, who loved spinach, always added butter and garlic.

I missed that dish. I missed my wife even more.

Wallakah had told me he had a son. Did he have a wife as well? Did the other Taliban members have wives? If so, what kind of lives did they lead?

I had my doubts that they were fulfilling. The Taliban expected their women to exist in isolation, cut off from education, technology, and any relationships outside of family networks. They were expected to completely cover their faces and bodies when in public. During the Taliban regime, they were forbidden to work, to leave the house without a male escort, or to seek medical help from a male doctor. Essentially, they had no rights. They could almost be considered slaves.

In the cities in modern Afghanistan, the situation for women was slowly changing. Women now had the right to vote. Some were going to school and working. A few had even achieved positions in government. Attitudes were definitely shifting, even if gradually. Would the men I was with now ever be open to such changes? It was a discussion that would have to wait for another day.

Immediately after dinner our captors handed a blanket each to Rafiq, Farzad, and me. Mercifully, after close to thirty hours in captivity, it appeared we would finally be allowed to get some real sleep.

I chose a spot near the wall at the far left side of the room, zipped up my jacket, and pulled on my hood. My trusty backpack would serve as my pillow.

I smiled at the sight of that green Eddie Bauer bag. It had been with me on my world travels for nearly two decades. Even the memory of receiving it was special.

On my twentieth birthday a friend had driven me to a college campus in Pasadena, supposedly to meet my parents. When I entered the college cafeteria, however, I was shocked by two hundred friends and family shouting, "Surprise! Happy birthday!" My parents and sister had been planning the party for weeks without revealing a thing to me. Of the many gifts I received that night, the one that endured the longest was the backpack presented by a friend named Richard, who was a mentor and my boss at USC at the time.

It was comforting to look at my backpack now and recall so many wonderful people and memories. As I laid my head on it, I was thankful to have something tangible to connect me to my life back home.

Above me was a one-foot square opening in the mud-and-stone wall. From my angle on the floor I couldn't actually see the night sky, but I could imagine the majesty and vastness of stars that shone brightly in the darkness. For a day spent with kidnappers and murderers, this one had turned out unexpectedly positive. I still had hope.

God, I prayed silently, *please redeem this situation as only you can.*

As I began to fall asleep and my thoughts drifted to places far away, the reality of my situation still tugged at me. I squirmed as I tried to avoid the rock digging into my upper back. My last sight before closing my eyes was of Kalashnikovs resting against a corner wall and against the pole in the middle of the room.

A PRECARIOUS PEACE

CHAPTER ELEVEN

6:00 A.M., FRIDAY, DECEMBER 7

THE DIM LIGHT OF DAWN HAD JUST BEGUN TO STEAL THROUGH the cracks in the two ventilation openings and doorway of our room when I yawned and opened my eyes. I felt so good. *Man,* I thought, *did I just sleep that long?*

It was more than just being rested. I had an incredible sense of peace, both physical and spiritual. I felt as if I were literally wrapped in a blanket of tranquility. The sensation was so strong that I actually lifted my arm and checked to see if there was something on top of me besides my blanket.

Even the thought of death could not disturb my new serenity.

If I am to die today, I'll still feel good that I connected well with my captors yesterday. What's the worst that can happen? I'll get shot and meet my creator a bit sooner than I expected. I'm okay with that.

What I didn't know then was that during the night—daytime Thursday in the States—my extended family, friends, and colleagues had begun to find out about my predicament. Many of these people immediately started praying for me, and some of them contacted national and international prayer networks. By the time I woke up, thousands of people around the world had asked God, on my behalf, to protect and safely deliver Rafiq, Farzad, and me from captivity.

Had I realized what was happening, I would have been humbled beyond measure. As it was, I simply reveled in the calm that enveloped me.

Am I still in captivity? I turned my head to take in the room. Yes, the stirring bodies of my captors, along with their Kalashnikovs, were all still here. Though I felt like a new man on the inside, my outer circumstances had not changed.

What I didn't know was that change was indeed on its way.

While we ate our usual breakfast of naan dipped in hot tea, the supply guy in the checkered headscarf returned. He was accompanied by a man I hadn't seen before. This one was older, probably in his midthirties, and had a short, neatly trimmed black beard. He was dressed in an all-black *salwar kameez*, a color more commonly seen in Pakistan or especially India. Unlike the supply guy, he definitely took notice of me. He didn't say anything, but when he entered the room, he gave me a long, intense look.

After breakfast Wallakah and Haqqani led Rafiq, Farzad, and me to a nearby hill. Wallakah handed me a cell phone and said, "Call your guys."

This time we got through to Roy. I explained how our signal had been cut off the day before. I also told him about the long conversation and connection with Wallakah during the previous afternoon.

"Even so, my feeling is that they still want to see a resolution in the next day or two," I said, "or something will happen." I didn't want to say what that "something" might be.

"Dilip, this just isn't going to resolve quickly," Roy answered. "We need time."

What Roy didn't say, but what I read between the lines, was that no one was going to come up with three hundred thousand dollars for our release. I'd already concluded as much.

Roy also introduced me to another voice on the line: Dean. He was a private negotiator our NGO had hired to help guide them. That sounded fine to me—having a professional involved couldn't hurt.

When our call ended, Wallakah asked what we'd talked about. I said only that I'd explained why we weren't able to connect the afternoon before. I left out the news about the private negotiator. Wallakah seemed satisfied with my answer.

A new character joined our troupe after our return to the shelter. The man who walked into our room was only about five foot two. He was probably in his fifties, with a dark complexion and a full but short black beard.

I was stunned. I'd seen this man somewhere before.

He seemed to know Rafiq. "Doctor *sahab, salaam alaikum* [sir, peace be upon you]," he said to him. He also greeted me, though I doubted he recognized me.

Then I remembered. He was a mullah—a local religious leader. He had represented the Taliban when Rafiq and I met with him and local police officials two years earlier, shortly after the opening of our education center in Pul-i-assim. We wanted to talk with them about how we could best serve the local population and also keep our staff secure. The mullah responded then that we were welcome to work and serve there, though the intention may have been to appear cooperative rather than actually be so.

Because the Taliban had almost no contact with our staff and deeply distrusted anyone foreign, animosity was bound to grow. They had kidnapped and killed several people east of Kabul during the previous two years, many of them Afghan construction workers led by foreign project directors. The Taliban had even harassed, abducted, or killed local government workers because of their links to foreign governments. For the citizens of this country, simply associating with foreigners was dangerous business.

In an attempt to be careful, I'd already canceled trips to the area because of these attacks. Obviously I hadn't been careful enough.

Seeing the mullah now angered me. How could he greet us so casually, as if running into people he'd met before and who were now hostages was routine? What upset me most was the difference in our worldviews. I viewed our situation as a crisis. To the mullah, this was just how business was done. It was a typical scene for him.

It bothered me, but I had to let it go. My day had started so well. I didn't want this incident to disrupt my sense of peace.

The mullah's arrival altered the casual, relaxed atmosphere of the previous day. Suddenly everyone was active. Wallakah and Ahmed gathered our blankets into one large bundle while the others picked up loose items. I didn't know where or why, but we were moving again.

We walked up and down more mountains. Based on the position of the sun, I thought we might be heading east, but I wasn't certain. We hiked about ninety minutes until we reached a plateau that lay between two hills. It was a space about twenty feet long, steep on both sides, with a trail that wound higher up the mountain ahead. Our only view was behind us on the trail we'd just walked, which revealed a mostly brown valley. A gust whistled through this opening, causing me to shudder. I guessed that our elevation was about five thousand feet.

While blankets were placed on the ground and we settled in, the mullah climbed the steep bank to our right for another four hundred feet, followed by Ahmed. The mullah sat atop a rock, apparently to make a phone call. I wondered whom he was calling.

Using leaves and twigs, our captors built a small fire. Not long after a serving of tea, a rare sound drifted up from the valley below— the whine of a motorbike's engine. I couldn't have been the only one who heard it, but no one else reacted to the noise. It seemed to be expected.

What, I wondered, was happening now?

The answer arrived soon enough. Our company was growing.

Two men marched into the middle of our camp. The first was probably in his early- or midthirties. He was tall and lanky, with a well-groomed beard that extended about two inches past his chin.

"Hello!" he said in Pashto. "How is everybody doing?"

When the rest of our group saw or heard this man, they immediately dropped what they were doing and focused their attention on him. Though he made no effort to intimidate and even smiled during his greetings, I realized he must be a Taliban leader.

While this man did not come across as scary, I was uneasy at the sight of the man who accompanied him. It was a familiar and definitely unsmiling face: the Butcher.

The new leader, whom the others addressed as the Commander, discussed matters with our captors. Within five minutes of his arrival, he turned to the three of us hostages and said via Rafiq's translation, "We are going to resolve all this in the next two hours."

Two hours? I felt my stomach tighten. This could be good, but it seemed more likely that a quick resolution would not be in our favor.

Whatever we were headed for, there was no doubt that events

were picking up speed. After lunch, six of us made a brief hike up the mountain: the Commander, the Butcher, Wallakah, and Hopeless, along with Rafiq and me. All the Taliban in this group were armed, except the Commander.

The Commander pulled a business card from his pocket, punched a number into another phone, and then handed the phone to me. "Talk to this guy," he said.

"Who am I going to talk with?" I asked. The Commander didn't answer.

"Hello?" I said into the phone.

"Hello," said a male voice. "I just want to commend you for your work." The speaker's accent identified him as Afghan, but he spoke good English. A friend of the Commander's, I assumed.

The man asked me a series of personal questions: "Where do you live in the States? How many children do you have? What are their names?"

I answered the questions but grew increasingly uncomfortable. "Who am I speaking with again?" I said.

"That's not important," the man said abruptly.

The questions continued, but I became more careful with my answers. I didn't want to endanger my family by giving too much information to the Taliban.

Then another voice came on the line—to my surprise, one that sounded American. "Dr. Joseph, this is Mark at the ISAF headquarters." ISAF was the International Security Assistance Force, a NATO-sponsored military presence in Afghanistan, made up of troops from the United States and other nations.

I exhaled with relief.

"Mark, it's such a pleasure to talk to someone from the States," I said. "If that was your colleague, I need to let you know that I gave him some coded answers because I didn't know who I was speaking with."

"That's all right," he said. "We just wanted to confirm who you are."

I passed more information on to Mark.

"You've done a good job of staying calm," he said. "Keep doing what you're doing. We have our eyes on you. Now I have someone else here who wants to talk to you."

A moment later a crisp voice filled my ear. "Hello, Dilip. I'm one of the generals here," a man said. "I just want to give you one tip: keep playing your Asian cards more than your American cards."

"General, thank you, I've been doing that."

Suddenly I heard only silence. We'd lost the signal.

I handed the phone back to the Commander. "Who were you talking to?" he demanded.

"It's your phone," I said. "You dialed it. I thought it was one of your friends." I certainly wasn't going to tell him that I'd just spoken with ISAF headquarters.

I guessed that the Commander didn't have any idea who he'd just put me in touch with, that calling the ISAF was simply random luck. My theory seemed even more likely a moment later when the Commander pulled the same business card from his pocket and asked if I recognized any of the phone numbers scribbled all over it. There must have been more than twenty. After taking a quick look, I said no.

Only later did I think of the possibility that the ISAF had intercepted the call so they could talk to me.

Either way, that phone conversation left me feeling more encouraged and less alone. The military knew where we were. Suddenly the idea of a rescue seemed a little less far-fetched.

A couple of minutes later the Commander again addressed his

hostages. "Here's how we're going to resolve this," he said. "We're going to exchange the three of you for four prisoners at Pul-e-Charkhi prison."

Wait a second, I thought. We were so focused on the money before. This was a new emphasis. *Are these guys communicating with each other? Is there going to be an argument over this?*

No one challenged the Commander's statement. I tried to stay positive. The prison was close to Kabul. Maybe if we were transferred there, someone from our staff in the city would be able to get us out.

Maybe.

The Commander handed me a phone and instructed me to call our team. At the same time, the Butcher caught my eye and traced a finger across his throat, a not-so-subtle reminder of what would happen if negotiations didn't succeed.

I reached Roy and Dean, though the connection was shaky and I had trouble hearing them. I explained how our Taliban numbers were growing and described the call with the ISAF. Then I related the new urgency and the new demand.

I suddenly remembered a comment Haqqani had made the day before—if we came up with two hundred thousand dollars quickly, then he, Wallakah, Hopeless, and Ahmed would divide the money among themselves and their families and let us go. I hadn't thought much about it at the time since so many numbers and demands were being thrown around. It was clear now, however, that with more players involved, our situation was growing more complicated.

I recalled something else—Haqqani's warning that Taliban from Pakistan would take us away if we couldn't resolve the situation quickly. I'd heard of abductions that had played out this way. Even after a ransom was paid, hostages were given to or "stolen" by another group, and the negotiation process started all over again.

I certainly did not want to end up in the lawless region that was western Pakistan. Were we near there even now? If we had indeed been traveling east, we might already be only a few miles from the border.

"Roy," I said, "this is moving in exactly the direction that they predicted. More Taliban are arriving, and the stakes are going up. I hope you will be able to respond."

"You know we're going to do everything on this end that we can, Dilip."

A crackle filled my ear, followed by silence. I'd lost the connection.

SHIFTING DEMANDS

I CONTINUED TO TRY TO REACH ROY AGAIN, WITHOUT SUCcess. Finally I gave up.

The Commander seemed in no hurry to change our position. Hands behind his back, he chatted with Wallakah, who sat on a large rock. Rafiq also stood close to the group. The Butcher, meanwhile, paced nearby. Then he sat down, pulled his knife from his waistband, and took off the black leather cover. He began using it to pick dirt from his fingernails, twisting it this way and that. The curved blade must have been about ten inches long, but at that moment it looked at least twenty.

To distract myself from disturbing thoughts, I approached Hopeless, who stood on a slope at the edge of our high point. Earlier I'd noticed both he and the Butcher occasionally pulling a thin nut off one of the Black Mountain bushes that surrounded us, then chewing on the nut. These tall bushes looked almost like trees. Their thin branches were covered with dull-green leaves with sharp, pointed tips. The nuts were smaller and rounder than a walnut, encased in a shell.

I pointed to one of the bushes then moved my hand to my mouth, pretending to chew. "Do you guys eat these?" I said to Hopeless, knowing full well he didn't speak English.

He seemed to grasp my meaning. He grabbed a branch of one of the bushes with one hand and plucked a nut off the branch with the other. Then he tore off the shell, muttering what probably could have been translated as, "You have to crack this open." He offered me the nut.

I tried it. There was almost no flavor. It must have made up in nutrition what it lacked in taste.

It was about this time that the distant sound of a single-engine airplane reached my ears. My eyes combed cloudy skies for a sign of it, with no luck. Was someone up there looking for us? Why else would someone fly a small plane in this forsaken territory?

The Commander interrupted my searching, breaking away from his conversation with Wallakah and turning to me.

"So do you like us?" he asked. "Are we treating you okay?"

"Like" was a relative term. I liked that they were feeding us and hadn't killed any of us yet.

"You guys seem okay," I said. "I'm okay with everybody except this guy." I nodded at the Butcher and smiled, trying to indicate it was a joke—sort of. Rafiq helped by laughing during his translation.

All the others chuckled in response, including the Commander. All, that is, but the Butcher.

The Commander finally decided it was time to move off the high point and back to the others at the plateau. The distance was only about a hundred feet, but it took us nearly ten minutes. Because of the uneven terrain, we had to stop several times to help one another.

At the plateau we were served another round of tea. While most of us sat and sipped from our glasses, the Commander stood and addressed me again. The question this time was more personal and far more dangerous: "Do you believe in God?"

I was startled, yet I'd also been anticipating something along this line since Rafiq and I had discussed it during the original long hike.

Here we go, I thought. *This could be the question that makes or breaks me.*

I had already resolved that, if asked, I would not lie about my faith. But I'd also decided to be wise about what I said. This wasn't the time for a theological debate. My purpose in Afghanistan was to love and care for its people.

My answer was short and to the point. "Ever since I was little," I said, "I have always believed in the one true God."

"Okay," the Commander said, his expression stern. "That's good. But I can look up your information on the Internet. If you're lying to us, we will kill you."

"That's fine if you want to look," I said. "If you're asking about my faith in God, that's exactly what I believe. I pray to the one true God, the almighty creator of the universe."

I wondered where this statement might lead. But instead of pressing me further about my faith, the Commander switched to more practical matters. It was time for our next phone call.

Back on our high point, I had no trouble this time connecting with Roy and Dean. They wanted more details on the prisoner exchange.

"Ask them," Dean said, "to give us the names of the four prisoners."

I pulled the phone from my ear. "Our guys are ready to move forward with this negotiation," I said to the Commander. "What are the names of the prisoners?"

The Commander didn't hesitate. In a matter-of-fact tone, he said,

"We're not going to do that now. We've changed the plan. We want three hundred thousand dollars, nothing less."

What?

Were they playing games? Testing us somehow? Or had they talked it over and decided to focus on the money after all?

I was especially frustrated at the thought they might be probing their ability to manipulate us. It occurred to me that I had leverage too. These guys needed my cooperation to get their demands met.

I gathered my courage and said as firmly as I could to the Commander, "We need to stick to one demand, or I can't communicate effectively."

When Rafiq translated, the Commander simply nodded. At least he didn't seem offended by my statement.

I relayed the latest change to Roy and Dean. They accepted the new direction with little comment, which made me think they'd expected all along that money was the real goal of our kidnappers. We agreed to talk again in the morning.

"How soon do you think they will get the money?" the Commander asked after I ended the call. "How soon will this all happen?"

Once again I needed to be careful. "Listen, we have to take this one day at a time," I said. "I've told them that you are now asking for three hundred thousand. They are working on it from their side. We will see what they say tomorrow morning."

This seemed to satisfy him.

Our communications with the outside world were done for the day. Now the Commander had other things on his mind. Back at the plateau he smiled slightly at me and said, "What would you like to have for dinner tonight?"

It was a question I hadn't expected. "I don't need anything special," I said. "You guys have been treating me just fine already."

"No, you are our guest," he said. "We are going to treat you to a feast tonight. We are going to kill a sheep in your honor."

"No, no, please don't go to all that trouble," I said. "You don't have to kill anything on my behalf. I'm good with what I've been eating."

This time several of the Taliban responded. "No, no, no," they said almost in unison.

"It's our duty to treat you and give you a feast in your honor as our guest," Wallakah said.

I suspected the feast was less about honoring their "guest" and more about coercing a local family to provide a good meal for our captors.

"Tomorrow you are going to make us a lot of money," the Commander said. "We want to give you a feast." Clearly I was not going to win this argument.

Our captors gathered up the blankets, kettle, tea, and sugar on the plateau. I noticed that another member had joined our group. This man appeared young, though it was difficult to tell since only his eyes were visible behind the scarf wrapped around his head and face. One of the others referred to him as a mullah, which seemed odd, considering he had a Kalashnikov strapped to his back. Nevertheless, I began to think of him as "Junior Mullah."

For the next hour we hiked downward toward a valley. *Where*, I wondered, *are we going? This is taking a long time.*

I surveyed the vast, arid plain that surrounded us. If someone was considering a rescue, this would be a bad place to try it. There was nowhere to hide.

The sun had just begun to set when we reached the base of the mountain, which connected with the valley floor. About a mile ahead, a dark object rose from the lowland, like a lonely grave. As we got closer, I saw that it was a two-story building, two windows with light emanating from within on the left and a single covered window on the right. Unlike most Afghan homes, it had no stone walls to indicate property boundaries. Apparently it was so isolated that boundaries weren't needed.

The owner of the house came out to greet us. I wondered if he was a cattleman—what other business could he operate way out here? He seemed to recognize some of our party and invited us in, shaking our hands as we entered. He had a light brown complexion and wore a white skullcap called a *taqiyah*. He was probably in his late forties or early fifties, though with his white beard and lined face, he looked to be in his late sixties.

I wondered if he knew that three of his guests were hostages.

We crowded into a living room that was roughly eight by fifteen feet. There were fifteen of us now—the house elder and his son, ten Taliban, and Rafiq, Farzad, and me. I realized we must have acquired yet another Taliban during our hike here because a slender young man with a scraggly beard and a *pakol* on his head now spoke with the Commander.

Some of the Taliban had stacked their guns in the corridor, but others carried their weapons right into the home, keeping them out of sight by stuffing them under the cushions that we began to sit on. The AK-47s were the elephants in the room—we all knew they were there. In most cultures it wouldn't be considered polite to bring assault rifles into a home. Security concerns apparently trumped manners on this night.

As we sat facing one another in a rectangle and talked, "Senior

Mullah" broke out a package of candy and passed it around. The mint gum treats came in shiny green wrappers with the label "Fresh & Cool."

Sweets were a symbol of celebration in this culture. I found the mullah's act odd. There was nothing to celebrate, at least not yet. Even so, I popped one into my mouth and tucked the empty wrapper into my pocket. It would be another souvenir from this experience—I hoped.

A minute later the need for security was underlined when I again recognized, above the buzz of conversation, the sound of a small plane somewhere overhead. The Commander must have heard it, too, because shortly after he wanted to talk about phone call surveillance.

"Do you know anything about it?" he asked me. "How do they listen in? Do you know anything about the satellite, how they track people?"

"I'm not an engineer," I said. "My area is medicine. I am not well versed in these things." I wondered why he thought I'd tell him even if I did know.

Our host sat at one end of the rectangle, near the doorway. Suddenly he threw a handful of medicine tablets onto the blanket in the middle of the room and began talking, an unhappy grimace on his face.

Apparently the Commander didn't appreciate this interruption. "Shh," he said. "Don't speak."

To my surprise, most of the other Taliban spoke up to defend the house elder. "No," more than one said. "This is his house. Let him speak." I found it interesting that even though the Commander was clearly in charge, his authority was not so ironclad that it prevented the others from disagreeing with him.

While this was going on, I reached out and picked up a couple of the tablets. They were ordinary antihistamines.

The elder, perhaps having heard that there were doctors present, explained that he suffered from itching all over his body. That morning, the itching on his scalp was so bad that he couldn't stand it anymore. He'd shaved his head. He took off his *taqiyah* to show us his bald pate.

"I am not at peace," he said loudly, raising his hands in the air. Our host said that on the one hand, he was expected to appease the local government. On the other hand, the Taliban were pressuring him to be on their side.

I was moved by this man's boldness. I didn't know the elder's business, but it was certainly possible that the government required bribes for him to conduct his affairs even while the Taliban demanded *Zakah*. He was in a predicament shared by too many of his countrymen.

One of my great passions was encouraging people to take a holistic view of their lives. Rather than the typical Western, allopathic model of identifying a health problem and then treating only the superficial symptoms of that problem, I advised looking at the combination of the physical, intellectual, emotional, and spiritual to get at the root issues. The elder's constant itching appeared to be a classic example of this. It seemed to me that the stress of his situation was showing up as a skin problem.

I admired this man's courage in sharing his frustration in front of my captors. It inspired me to speak up as well.

"I want you to know that our creator God, the God of this universe, is a God of peace," I said to the elder. Everyone had been talking, but as soon as I began to speak, they stopped. While Rafiq translated, it was quiet enough to hear a snake slither.

"I regret that you feel caught between the government authorities and the Taliban factions and find it difficult to appease both parties. In fact, you are right. You can't satisfy both sides."

Man, I thought, *they might just shoot me right now.* Yet the room remained completely still, everyone focused on my words and Rafiq's translation.

You could say that I had a captive audience.

"Our God actually cares so much about us," I continued, "that he will direct our ways so that we can make decisions that lead to peace. You never have to worry about a decision you need to make, whether it is the right one or wrong one because he will direct your steps."

The elder nodded his head at me.

"It is my hope and prayer that you can make the right decisions so that you don't have to deal with this itching anymore," I said.

The group went back to their conversations without any dialogue with me. I didn't know if my words had made an impression or not. Still, just like my speech during the long first hike about my wife's Pashtun background, I at least had the satisfaction of knowing that I had tried to connect and had expressed my views.

The feast, on the other hand, was less than satisfying. We divided into groups of four that gathered in circles around our food. Somehow I ended up next to the Butcher. Our meal turned out to be a half-cooked lamb and a spinach dish. The lamb tasted as if it had been boiled in water but not actually cooked. The Taliban gorged on it. They couldn't get enough.

I could barely stand it, however. I managed to finish one piece of meat and a bit of naan. Between the taste and my lack of enthusiasm for what this party stood for, I'd lost my appetite.

The Butcher noticed. Apparently he felt I wasn't eating fast enough, as he motioned for me to eat more. "Keep eating, keep eating," he said. "Be full."

I made a show of putting more lamb into my mouth. A moment later, not wanting to lose this rare opportunity to connect with my nemesis, I tapped the Butcher on his shoulder and patted my stomach, letting him know I was full. He didn't react, but at least he didn't seem to mind the interruption.

After more sweets, tea, and conversation, it was time to go. The house elder stood at the edge of the courtyard as the Taliban lined up, shaking hands with each as they departed.

When my turn came, our host clasped my hand in both of his. His dark brown eyes looked intently into mine. Since I hadn't spoken any Pashto throughout the evening, I figured he'd realized by now that I was a hostage. I sensed his compassion. If he spoke English, I think he would have said, "Thank you for honoring me with your presence. Good luck."

"*Tashakor*," I said, which was "thank you" in Dari, Afghanistan's other official language.

It must have been about eight o'clock when we left the elder's home. I wondered where we were headed now. I certainly hoped we weren't embarking on another all-night walk. As we moved up and down trails, several of the Taliban used the flashlight feature on their cell phones, swinging them back and forth to light their way in the darkness. As they hiked along in their sandals and *salwar kameezes*, I pondered the odd mix of centuries-old tradition and new technology.

"Shh!"

The universal signal for silence came from somewhere up ahead.

At the same time, someone else hissed a command in Pashto, probably "Keep quiet!" Everyone around me froze.

We'd been hiking without incident for about forty-five minutes. What had changed?

Wallakah pointed at Rafiq, Farzad, and me, and then at the ground. We sat. He trained his AK-47 on me.

Could this be it? Had the military arrived? Was someone trying a rescue effort?

I stared at Wallakah, his eyebrows furrowed and lips pinched together, his attention on what was happening ahead of us, his finger on the trigger of the weapon pointed at my head.

This is Wallakah, the guy I've connected with. Surely he's not going to pull the trigger? Yet he's the one with the gun aimed right at me.

Ah, this is going to be a royal mess. Everybody's going to be shot or hurt or killed. And I'm going to be the first one.

Then as quickly as the crisis formed, it ended. Whatever had spooked the front of the line—an animal? another member of the Taliban?—must have been identified. I exhaled and got up. We resumed our hike.

We'd walked only another couple hundred feet when to my surprise the two-story mud house with the outdoor pool of water came into view. We'd returned to the same area where we'd spent the last two nights.

Everyone stopped at the pool to wash their hands, face, and feet. I also washed my hand and face. As I splashed water on myself, the black-clad Talib sidled next to me.

"Hey," he said quietly in broken Urdu, the official language of Pakistan, "do you drink? Want some liquor?" To make sure I understood, he put his thumb to his mouth and tipped his head back.

I shook my head. "No," I said, waving my hand in front of me.

"Do you want a smoke?" He put two fingers to his lips. "I can get you one."

"No, thank you," I said in English.

I noticed he had blackened lips, obviously from smoking. The idea that this man apparently smoke and drank surprised me a bit, considering that he was part of a fundamentalist group. But at the same time I wasn't that surprised. I'd come across many extremists who had figured out loopholes for nearly every religious belief.

After getting permission to walk away from the group to urinate, I walked about a hundred feet away from the others to do so. I was uneasy. Our little group had swelled to three captives and ten Taliban. I felt little connection to most of our captors and had no idea what would happen next.

Suddenly I realized what I was doing. A chill dropped down my spine, like a bead of sweat. *My back is turned to these guys. And nearly all of them have guns.*

I was again afraid of offending the Taliban and having my life end in a most humiliating manner. Despite the difficulty, I crouched to finish my business.

Soon everyone gathered in front of the mosque. We had to wait to bed down, however. In someone's careless haste to warm up everyone's blankets for the night, one had caught fire, filling the shelter with smoke. Many of the others—even Rafiq and Farzad—used the opportunity to get on their knees for *namaz*.

I sat against a wall outside the entrance. It was a lonely moment. When and how was this all going to end? I said another prayer.

I wanted to go home.

Finally the haze cleared enough for us to enter the shelter. As we did, the distant sound of an engine reached our ears for the third time that day. There might even have been more than one.

I didn't think the Commander would be pleased. I was right.

"You hear those planes?" he said to me, looking up and pointing skyward. "If they are coming for you, we are going to kill the three of you first because we know we're going to die anyway."

I didn't respond. What was there to say?

Bedtime came quickly. With thirteen of us lying on the ground, we were packed into the room like sardines. I arranged my backpack once again as a pillow and pondered the Commander's words.

I'd been threatened so many times in the last three days that this latest warning did not add a fresh wave of terror. After all, these guys were desperate for money, and to get their money they needed me alive. On the other hand, if things started to go south, emotions could get in the way of logic. They easily could end up pulling the trigger.

I said another prayer, closed my eyes, and began to fall into a fitful sleep. Saturday was going to be a big day.

"PAPA'S IN TROUBLE"

THURSDAY, DECEMBER 6
COLORADO SPRINGS, COLORADO

BACK IN THE UNITED STATES, TWO PEOPLE I WAS VERY CLOSE to also were not sleeping well—my wife and sister.

It had been a rough two days for Cilicia. She had taken Daniel's advice to heart and said nothing about my abduction to anyone, not even her father. Keeping that news to herself, along with her fears and concerns, was among the hardest things she'd ever had to do.

She'd been told I was alive, of course, and about the ransom demands. But she also knew that the demands were so outrageous that there was virtually no chance they would be met.

Our children were still going to school. Cilicia didn't want them to worry, so she didn't fill them in. But Asha and Jaron, in particular, realized that something was up. "We just need to pray for Papa," was all Cilicia would say. "Papa's in some kind of trouble."

On Thursday a woman named Mary called Cilicia from the FBI office in Washington, D.C. She reassured Cilicia that the FBI, the state department, and the ISAF were aware of the situation and were working together to secure my release, though she didn't provide details.

My sister, Deepa, meanwhile, was alarmed. About two o'clock Thursday morning, the U.S. State Department in Kabul had called and left a message at her Los Angeles home. They wanted to verify that she was my sister, but the caller didn't explain further. It left her scared and wondering what was going on.

Cilicia received another call from the FBI that day. This agent informed her that preparations for a military rescue were underway. Before they could act, however, they needed her to sign a form. It would give the government permission to attempt the rescue—and release it from any legal responsibility if things turned out badly.

Cilicia didn't know what to do. Was it better to try to negotiate or attempt a dangerous rescue? What created the greatest chance of bringing me home? She called my boss, Daniel, for advice.

For the remainder of Thursday, Cilicia was in almost-constant contact with Daniel, Mary, or Lars, Morning Star's executive director, as they talked through the latest updates and options. All of them were a steady source of support, answering her questions and providing a measure of comfort and peace despite the dire circumstances. Mary also called Deepa, filling her in and leaving her feeling at least a little hopeful that she might see her brother again. Later that day Cilicia and Deepa connected by phone and text. They encouraged each other through their shared concern for me.

Yet a decision had to be made. Cilicia and Daniel both agonized over the choice before them. Some of the people advising Daniel recommended immediate military action. Others strongly pushed for continuing with negotiations.

Cilicia went to bed on Thursday night, my Friday morning in

Afghanistan, still uncertain about what to do. When she woke up in the middle of the night, she did what was natural for her—she turned to her Bible. As she sat in bed and flipped pages, she sensed God leading her to a passage:

> Do not be afraid of those who kill the body but cannot kill the soul. . . . Are not two sparrows sold for a penny? Yet not one of them will fall to the ground apart from the will of your Father. And even the very hairs of your head are all numbered. So don't be afraid; you are worth more than many sparrows.[1]

They were encouraging, peace-giving words. Cilicia realized that no matter what happened to my body, I had already dedicated myself to God. My soul was safe with him.

Suddenly Cilicia had the strong impression that it was going to be okay—that they should try for the rescue. She would talk with Daniel, but she already felt sure he would agree. They'd already discussed the idea of Daniel signing the government permission form for both of them. Now it was time. She would trust in her new feeling of assurance and in God.

Cilicia swung her legs out of bed, walked downstairs and into our dark kitchen, and opened up her laptop. It was two o'clock Friday morning in Colorado Springs, one thirty in the afternoon in Afghanistan. After a few keystrokes, she sent Daniel the following e-mail:

Hi Daniel,
Here is my formal authorization; please let me know if you need something different.

I will be waiting to hear the latest from you.

Thanks,

Cilicia

December 7, 2012, 2:00 a.m. MST

I, Cilicia Joseph, authorize Morning Star Development to make a decision(s) in the best interest of my husband, Dilip Joseph, to involve the U.S. State Department and/or other agencies.

Now all she could do was wait.

On Friday afternoon Cilicia heard a knock on our front door. She'd been expecting it. When she opened the door, she found a group of four men and women on our porch. Some carried bags or what looked like small suitcases.

"Mrs. Joseph?" said the man in front, showing an identification badge. "We're from the FBI. With your permission we'd like to come in and gather some of your husband's DNA samples."

Cilicia let them in and showed them to our bathroom upstairs. The FBI team took one of my old toothbrushes and hair samples from a clipper.

Left unspoken was the reason for gathering remnants of my DNA—if needed, a way to identify my body.

I met these two brothers during a visit to eastern Afghanistan. Their family and others wanted us to establish a community center for their villages.

My work includes teaching Afghan medical staff about communicable diseases.

Moms wait with their children for their turns to see the doctor at one of our rural health clinics.

Miriam, the midwife, used this display board as she talked with young mothers in Pul-i-assim about nutrition, family planning, pregnancy, and vaccinations.

One of our doctors sees patients at this Pul-i-assim medical clinic.

Kuchi nomads are leaving Pul-i-assim, bound for Kabul. This is the same road and quite close to the spot where we were abducted by the Taliban.

A pair of mujahideen stand watch in an area near Pul-i-assim.

This is a typical Afghan meal, which I share with village elders. It includes naan, chicken, rice, and vegetables. I am about to eat a slice of tomato.

The opulent appearance of this mosque in western Afghanistan is typical for a mosque in the city.

In a remote community in Kabul province, apricot trees grow in the foreground, the structure on the left is a school, and the building on the right is a home.

A verdant valley outside of Kabul City is a great reminder that well-managed resources produce tangible results.

Employers know they can find men looking for work on this bridge over the Kabul River.

Kuchi nomads make their living driving herds of sheep, goats, donkeys, and camels to the city. A single sheep may sell for as much as $250.

Darul Aman Palace, on the outskirts of Kabul, was constructed during the reign of King Amanullah Khan. Though its name means "abode of peace," it was virtually destroyed during battles among rival mujahideen factions in the early 1990s.

My coauthor, Jim Lund, walks the streets of Kabul, March 2014.

Many of the streets of Kabul are lined with vendors
selling fruit and all types of wares.

Afghans are endlessly creative in finding ways to carve homes
into whatever space is available, as on this hillside in Kabul.

These snow-capped mountains surround Kabul.

Kids play soccer in the street in Kabul with whatever
is available—in this case, a basketball.

The future of Afghanistan is in her people.

ON THE RUN

CHAPTER FOURTEEN

5:30 A.M., SATURDAY, DECEMBER 8
BLACK MOUNTAIN RANGE, AFGHANISTAN

SOME OF MY FAVORITE "PAPA" MOMENTS HAVE OCCURRED ON Saturday mornings. While sleeping soundly in my bed at home, I might suddenly be awakened by a small but warm body cuddling up next to me. Asha had mostly outgrown that, but Jaron and Tobi still loved to crawl into bed between Cilicia and me for a few minutes of cozy time to start the weekend. Seeing their obvious pleasure at being with us always brought me a generous measure of joy as well.

As I emerged from my slumber on this Saturday morning, I had the briefest hope that the kidnapping was a terrible dream, that I would wake up at home and find one of the boys quietly snuggling next to me, a shy smile on his face.

Instead, I awoke to the sound of voices chanting in Pashto.

I blinked a few times in the predawn darkness, trying to get oriented. Senior Mullah was on his knees, leading a time of *namaz*. Facing him in a row, all nine of the other Taliban, along with Rafiq and Farzad, were also on their knees, chanting prayers.

121

I was the only one still in "bed." I was actually embarrassed and wondered why they hadn't woken me.

Should I get up? Should I not? It's weird to lie here when everyone else is up praying.

I remembered that on Thursday, Wallakah had asked me, "Do you believe in prayer? Do you pray?"

"Absolutely I believe in prayer," I'd answered. "Prayer to me is having a conversation with our creator God." I'd then shown him how I prayed—on my knees, palms open, and eyes closed.

I decided to do the same thing now. I got on my knees right where I'd been sleeping and began to pray quietly: "Lord, you have been with me for the past three days. Give me the strength and courage to face today as well."

I could almost feel everyone's eyes on me. It was a little strange, all of us praying at the same time, though not quite in the same way. Yet it had a unifying feel. Despite all our differences, prayer was a pivotal part of life for every person in that room.

As soon as *namaz* ended, we all huddled in the front of the room. Haqqani and Wallakah started a fire to heat a kettle for tea. For the first couple of days, our seven glasses had been enough to go around. Now there were thirteen of us.

"You go ahead," I said when tea was poured and offered to me.

"No, you drink first," someone insisted. Hostage or not, the custom of serving guests first still prevailed. I sipped quickly, knowing that others were waiting for their turn to drink.

After draining my tea and while the others talked and were served, I asked to go outside to relieve myself. I was grateful that Wallakah was the one who offered to go with me.

As I crouched in the cool, cloudy morning, I again heard the sound of a plane. I couldn't see who was up there, but it sure seemed that someone was trying to track us. Was there a plan? With the three of us surrounded by so many armed Taliban, was there any chance of getting out of this alive? I realized there was no point in trying to figure out the details. I had no control over it.

Wallakah and I walked silently back to the shelter. Just outside the front door, a boy of about twelve held a large water jug with both hands. He'd just filled the jug that sat outside the shelter.

Wallakah, smiling, gestured at the boy. "Mujahideen—training," he said to me. There was a hint of pride in his voice.

I was surprised and pleased to meet a young man. He was about four and a half feet tall and slim, with smooth features. My first instinct was to extend my hand and shake his. When the boy raised his head and his eyes met mine, however, I was startled. His eyebrows were low and knotted, his lips pressed into a tight frown. It was a look of anger and hatred.

I tried not to react, but I felt anger rising in me as well—not at the boy but at his circumstances. As with the boy who brought us water during the long hike on Wednesday, I wondered if the Taliban had taken over this youth's life and poisoned his thoughts, filling him with hatred for anyone foreign. Or was he angry about his lack of opportunities, the education and freedoms he would never experience?

I nodded at the youth and stepped past him to wash my hands and face. Compassion and sadness mixed with my anger. This young man was not so much older than my own children, but his life was headed in a very different direction.

When I entered the shelter, I sensed another shift in our captors' attitude—more businesslike, more urgent. The casual conversations had ceased. No one was smiling. People were moving quickly and gathering up belongings.

I remembered Haqqani's early Thursday announcement that we had three days to meet their demands. This was the third day.

I noticed Rafiq and Farzad huddled in the corner, having a serious conversation. Before I could ask what they were discussing, we were all herded out the door.

The Butcher prodded me with his AK-47. We started walking to the left, toward the same mountain where we'd made calls the day before. Rafiq was next to me. The Commander also walked with us.

The rest of the group, however—including Farzad—moved to the right, toward the same area where we'd hiked the previous night.

My concern hit a new level.

We're separating. We're getting weaker as a unit. There are so many more Taliban than before. What's going to happen to Farzad? Will we ever see him again? What's going to happen to us? The captors we're with now are guys I haven't connected with—the Commander and the Butcher who's so threatening I can't even look at him.

This was truly grim.

As if to confirm my fears, Rafiq moved closer as we hiked and whispered, "Do you see what they're doing? They're separating Farzad from us. I don't like this at all."

Unlike the day before, this time we climbed all the way to the top of the mountain, which had a flat peak. It was warmer than previous mornings, probably in the forties. A smattering of clouds marred an otherwise blue sky. From here we could see for miles into the valley below.

The Commander gave me a phone. "Call your guys," he said.

Roy answered the phone immediately. "Let me give you a quick summary on what's happened since yesterday afternoon," I said to him. I explained about the growing Taliban numbers, about the feast, and how Farzad was no longer with us.

Suddenly the connection went dead.

Here we go again, I thought. I tried repeatedly to reconnect, without success. Finally I got through again. Roy turned the call over to Dean.

"Dilip, can you describe their attitude toward you?" Dean asked.

"It's been okay. So far."

"All right," he said. "I have a request for you. If possible, we'd like you to take a picture with your phone and send it to us."

"A picture?" I said.

"Yes. If you can show some of the mountain, the valley, and the angle of the sun, that would be extremely helpful."

I pondered this. I had my doubts that I could successfully pull this off. On the other hand, if I was discreet, it might work. I decided I had to try.

I disconnected the call but kept talking, pretending that my conversation was continuing. I also told Rafiq what I planned to do so he could focus even more than usual on keeping the Commander and the Butcher occupied.

Now I frowned at the phone and walked in a circle, acting as if I was having trouble with the reception. I ended up in a spot about thirty feet away from the rest of the group.

I found the camera application on the phone. When I thought no one was looking, I quickly lined up a shot and pressed the "take picture" button.

On my phone the picture process is a silent one. That was what I expected on the Commander's phone. When I pressed the button, however, I was horrified to hear the sound that an old-fashioned camera makes—a loud *click*.

The Butcher noticed it immediately.

"Did you just take a picture?"

My heart started pumping double-time. "No," I said. "Not that I know of."

I quickly switched the phone from camera to call mode. The Butcher rushed over and snatched the phone from my hand. He pressed buttons until he found the images stored on the phone, including the one I'd just shot.

"You did take a picture."

I fought off a feeling of rising panic and forced my voice to remain steady.

"Ah, I'm sorry," I said. "I think I might have pressed a button by mistake. I'm not used to this phone."

The Butcher deleted the image and glared at me but said nothing else.

That was that. I wasn't going to try any more photos. I wondered if I'd just pushed the Butcher's suspicions to a dangerous level.

A few minutes later, however, both of us forgot all about the phone call. We were sitting about twenty-five feet from the edge of the plateau. At the sound of an engine, all four of us turned our heads toward the valley.

Some five miles away, a dust cloud rose from the plains floor. It was created by a black Hilux and a motorcycle that followed behind it. They were crossing the lowland, moving from our left to our right.

We watched in silence for the next minute. Then the vehicles stopped. Human figures poured out of the doors and bed of the truck, perhaps fifteen of them. Many held long objects that certainly looked like weapons.

"Those are representatives from the Pakistani Taliban commission in Waziristan," the Commander said, standing quickly. "They're coming to take you."

Haqqani had predicted this would happen. I couldn't believe his words were coming true.

The Butcher had also leapt to his feet. He beckoned sharply to Rafiq and me with his arm. "Move!" he said. "Run!"

Our captors ducked their heads as we ran, apparently worried about being seen. It didn't make sense to me. If the men in the valley were Taliban, why were these guys running away? But I wasn't going to argue. I didn't want to end up with them either.

Suddenly I stopped. "My bag!" I said, pointing to where it sat next to a rock some sixty feet away. "I've left it behind."

That backpack meant a lot to me. If nothing else, I wanted to save it as a keepsake if I survived. I didn't want to lose it now.

Rafiq translated my words. The Butcher's agitated expression showed he had no desire to fetch this foreigner's luggage. But when the Commander uttered a few words, the Butcher scrambled back to our plateau and grabbed my backpack.

We ran, stooping, out of sight of the Hilux and its passengers until we reached the back side of the mountain. Then we slowed to a fast walk, moving down and away from the mountain. I couldn't help thinking of Farzad. Weren't we now going in the opposite direction of where he'd been headed?

For better or worse, it felt as if we were reaching the end of the line.

THE TALIBAN DRY MY TEARS

CHAPTER FIFTEEN

11:00 A.M., SATURDAY

OVER THE NEXT HALF HOUR, FEW WORDS WERE EXCHANGED. All of us were winded. We passed hills and sand dunes. Sweat formed on my brow and back. The temperature rose into the sixties, the sun's heat magnified by our exertions. My lips were parched. I was ready to drink anything, parasites or not.

I found relief in a different form, however, when we came around yet another hill. About a hundred feet ahead, moving in the same direction as the four of us, were the rest of our original group—including Farzad.

We hurried to catch up. The lack of surprise on the faces of the Taliban, and even on Farzad's face, told me that these guys had planned all along to link up again. But neither Rafiq nor I had known it. We were too out of breath to speak, but Rafiq's grin let me know he was as overjoyed as I was to be with our friend again.

Not for the first time, I was thankful that the three of us were going through this ordeal together. Rafiq had done much to relieve tension by talking frequently with our captors and keeping the conversation light. Farzad's steady demeanor also helped everyone stay calm emotionally. It meant everything to me. I couldn't imagine doing this on my own.

A few minutes later, as our narrow trail wound around another mountain, we came across a puddle of water. It was perhaps five feet long and three feet wide. Along with several of the others, I knelt down and dipped my hand to take a single sip. The cool water was so refreshing that I quickly dipped my hand in for more.

My "old friend" Hopeless was watching. After four sips, he'd seen enough. He motioned for me to get up and start hiking again. As I stood, he took a long look behind us, apparently to make sure no one was following. Though I didn't know why, we were still hurrying to get away from the other Taliban.

Our path grew steeper and became a climb as much as a hike. We drifted apart into groups of three or four, but I saw we were all aiming for the peak of the brown, barren mountain ahead. When the lead group was less than a hundred feet from the top, it stopped and waited for the others, including ours, to catch up. When we reached them, I rested in the shade provided by a twenty-foot-tall desert tree with small, dark green leaves. I had been breathing hard and was thankful for the respite.

From the position of the sun directly overhead, I guessed that it was noon when we reached the top of the mountain. The climb had been exhausting, but the view was impressive. For the first time in days, my eyes took in more than dusty hills and rocks. A long, wide valley opened up before us for perhaps ten miles. Dotted here and there were signs of life—plowed fields, homes, even villages. Three or four miles away, a road ran parallel to the horizon, adjoined by a river. On the far side of the valley, another mountain range stretched into the sky.

Rafiq, standing next to me, kept his head still but pointed with his eyes. "Do you now see where we are?" he whispered.

"Is that the Kabul-Jalalabad Highway?" I whispered back. "And the Kabul River?"

"Yes."

It was a relief to have at least some idea of our location.

The leaders of our group—including the Commander, the Butcher, Wallakah, and Haqqani—stood in a circle near the precipice and spent the next few minutes engaged in intense conversation. Senior Mullah claimed a spot on a large rock right at the edge and also chimed in at times. I didn't know what any of them were saying, of course, but my guess was they were deciding what to do next. The Commander also received a series of calls on his phone.

Once this conversation ended, the Commander walked over to me and handed me his phone. "Call your guys," he said.

I definitely felt the expectations of our captors in that moment. It was deadline day. If something didn't happen soon, we were in trouble.

It took me three tries to get through to Roy. When I did, he said, "Dilip, we're ready to negotiate. We also have a translator here."

I let out a long breath. This was a moment I'd hoped for and feared would never come. Somehow my colleagues, family, and friends must have scraped together enough funds to get this process moving.

"Great!" I said. "I'll hand over the phone."

I watched intently as the translator on Roy's end spoke to the Commander. The Commander relayed the message to Rafiq, who passed it on to me: "They are offering a ransom of nine thousand dollars."

What? Did I hear that right?

Rafiq confirmed it—nine thousand.

My first response wasn't exactly filled with grace or gratitude: *I can't believe I'm worth only nine thousand dollars!* Then I realized that the offer wasn't for me alone, but all three of us.

We're going to die. They're going to shoot us right now.

To my surprise, however, the Commander and the others didn't react to the offer with anger. "We are not backing down one penny from three hundred thousand," the Commander said. His tone was even, not confrontational. The phone conversation continued.

Hmm, I thought. *I guess this is how the game is played. No one expects a first offer to be accepted.*

As the negotiation went back and forth, it occurred to me that maybe a low offer was best after all. The less money that went into the hands of these insurgents, the better. I knew all too well how the funds might be used.

The Commander ended the call with Roy's team and launched into another long discussion with the rest of our captors. Beyond them was a steep decline into the wide valley below.

Wallakah caught my eye and placed his hand over his heart. A few minutes later, to my surprise, Ahmed did the same. I appreciated their reassuring gestures.

Then the Talib in black approached me. "Do you speak Urdu?" he asked in that language.

"Very little," I replied in Hindi, which is similar to Urdu. I comprehend Hindi pretty well and probably understood about 20 percent of spoken Urdu. It wasn't enough to carry on much conversation, but the fact that this Urdu guy had tried to communicate with me at all was encouraging.

The rest of the group, meanwhile, was ignoring me. The voices around the Commander grew louder. The Commander received more calls. Then Rafiq joined these talks, adding a considerable flow of words of his own. Every face was serious and tense.

They were discussing matters of life and death—probably mine. I desperately wished I knew what was being discussed.

Suddenly the Commander turned to me. "You need to speak to your organization, tell them we're serious about the three hundred thousand," he said. "This is exactly what we want."

The Commander's instructions were interrupted by another call. He frowned as he concentrated on the voice on the other end of the phone. When he finished the call, the Commander eyed me and made an announcement that Rafiq translated for me: "The Pakistani Taliban are offering us fifty thousand to hand you over to them. This is way more than your organization is offering us."

"Many NGOs, including ours, are small," I said. "They don't have extra money available to pay for emergencies like these."

The Commander waved his hand, cutting off Rafiq's translation, and went back to talking with the others.

I realized I was again fighting the common belief among Afghans that all foreigners and their NGOs are loaded with money. I remembered some of my past conversations with village elders. I'd explained that although we were there to help, they had to look at existing community assets to meet their needs rather than expect international donations to solve all their problems. I'd always tried to help the villagers understand the distinction between our role as a coach or guide and their responsibility to take ownership of the development process. The context was frighteningly different now, but the mind-set was similar—a group of rural Afghans was hoping to improve its lot with the aid of foreign money.

I wished I could befriend these guys and help them see a better way to live. That, after all, was one of the reasons why I came here—to help people view their situation through a fresh lens. *If only they could see their potential. Don't they realize they're leading a dead-end lifestyle?*

I watched the Commander from about fifteen feet away. The calm demeanor he'd demonstrated the last two days was slowly eroding as his phone continued to ring and discussions with the other Taliban heated up. He frowned more often and occasionally raised his arm to make a point. Some of the others also seemed more agitated as they raised their voices and paced back and forth. Not surprisingly, the two who appeared most frustrated were Hopeless and the Butcher.

The Commander waved me over. "We need to resolve this in the next few hours," he said via Rafiq, "or your situation is going to get much worse. The Pakistani Taliban are telling me to hand you over to them."

The tension and frustration were getting to me. How was any of this going to turn out well? I sat down in the dirt and covered my head with the hood of my jacket. The sun's heat reminded me of how tired and thirsty I was.

Lord, I prayed silently, head down, *there's no sign of any of this taking a turn for the good. Please, somehow, mend their hearts and move them toward a better idea.*

Suddenly something hard slammed into my right side just below my rib cage. Pain shot through me.

I twisted to look behind me. The Butcher stood there, pointing the butt of his AK-47 as if ready to strike again.

"Why did you do that?" I almost yelled. "What have I done to you?" He may not have understood my words, but I was sure he caught my meaning.

At the same time as my protest, a chorus of objections rose from the Taliban around us. I didn't need a translation to capture the gist of it: "Don't do that again!"

Shocked and angry as I was, I was also grateful that the others seemed to be on my side, at least at the moment.

The Butcher stepped away from me and calmed down, saying something back to the group. "He's really frustrated," Rafiq said to me, quietly. "He wants this to move along."

The Commander took charge. "Let's talk this through," he said while waving Rafiq over. The young man I thought of as his assistant also joined him, along with Haqqani and the Urdu guy.

They sat down on the large, flat rock at the edge of the precipice where Senior Mullah still sat. It must have been four feet tall and ten feet long. I thought about how easily that big rock could dislodge, sending them all tumbling down the mountain. But none seemed the least bit concerned. These men were used to living on the edge, in more ways than one.

From a distance of about ten feet, I watched the conversation for the next half hour and wondered what they were saying. I had no doubt that something was going to happen soon. In a sense, all of us were like a boulder that was rolling down the mountain, faster and faster. Before much longer our boulder had to either roll to a stop or hit something and blow apart.

As I sat and pondered this, I heard the now-familiar sound of a small airplane. I looked up and for the first time actually spotted it against a brilliant blue backdrop as it made one pass in the distance. I thought it might have been a Piper Cherokee. Whatever it was, I was thankful to see it and hoped someone friendly was watching us.

Unfortunately I wasn't the only one to notice the plane. Its appearance seemed to raise the intensity level among the Taliban. As they talked, their voices grew louder and their gestures more emphatic. Even Hopeless, who rarely said anything, joined in with an outburst.

Curious, I called out to Rafiq and asked what he'd said. He shook his head.

"He said that he's tired of all the talk," Rafiq said. "He said if someone will give him the command he will gladly finish us off."

I swallowed and wished I hadn't asked.

Not long after, Rafiq broke away from the conversation and whispered to me, "I've been trying to negotiate for them to release all three of us," he said. Then he sat back down with the Taliban.

Several minutes later everyone in the group stood. The Commander had Rafiq make a call. Since Rafiq spoke to the caller in English, I guessed that it was Roy or Dean. I moved closer.

After a few moments Rafiq covered the phone. His jaw tensed as he spoke.

"The Taliban are talking about releasing only me and Farzad to get money for you. Dean says we should go. But I will not leave you."

I didn't like the sound of this. I took the phone. "Dean, I'm really concerned about this idea they have of separating us."

"Dilip," he said, "this plan of Rafiq and Farzad leaving is a great idea."

A great idea? I'd be losing my friends, my translator, my only lifeline to our captors. I'd be totally alone.

"How could that possibly be a good idea? I wouldn't have any way of communicating with these guys. I don't think I can handle this on my own."

Dean's voice was calm and reassuring. "Trust me on this one, Dilip. This is the best thing that could happen to you."

I squeezed the phone tighter and tried to control my emotions. Dean was the professional. I wanted to believe him. But I did not want to be left alone with these people.

I took a deep breath. "I will have to trust you," I said. "But I don't understand this at all."

Moments after I ended the call with Dean, the Commander motioned Wallakah over to the rock and made a short speech. Whatever he said, Wallakah didn't like it. His voice grew louder, and his face reddened.

Then Wallakah started yelling at the top of his lungs. Most of it I couldn't understand, but one phrase was clear: "Pakistan madrassa! Pakistan madrassa!" The Commander, his expression neutral, raised his palms in an effort to calm Wallakah.

I realized that Wallakah was objecting to the plan of separating us, maybe also to his role in the new arrangement. He was more or less saying, "You guys don't know what you're doing. I don't want to be part of this anymore. I'm going to Pakistan to join a madrassa."

I put my hand over my heart and tried to catch Wallakah's eye. I wanted to communicate the same message that he'd given to me so many times these last three days: It's okay. Don't worry. It's going to work out.

A minute later Rafiq approached me. I saw the anguish on his face. He couldn't look me in the eyes.

"They have decided to separate us," he said. "I do not want to do this."

I didn't want him to do it either. I realized how terrible he felt about leaving me and feared for what was going to happen to all of us. But Dean had said this separation was a good idea.

And we had no choice.

"Go," I said, tears coming to my eyes. "Go to Roy and discuss with him what to do next."

"Dilip, whatever I have, I will sell it," Rafiq said. "I will raise the money. Any help that I can do."

Now it seemed everyone in the camp was stirring, preparing to move. Farzad walked over to Rafiq and me.

For the last three days I felt I'd been calm and strong, even at peace, despite being held hostage by dangerous insurgents and despite continual death threats. Now, however, I felt myself falling apart. I didn't see how I could get through this without the two friends who'd shared this ordeal with me. Would I ever see them again?

The Commander and some of the other Taliban moved toward the trail that led down the mountain. It was time to say good-bye. Because of our language barrier, there was little Farzad and I could say to each other. His eyes, however, communicated the same concern, compassion, and sadness that I felt. Rafiq, meanwhile, raised his head this time to look at me. I saw that his eyes had also welled up.

I slipped my backpack off of my shoulder and handed it to Rafiq. The Taliban had taken most of my possessions, but they'd left my medical lecture notes in the backpack. I'd worked hard to refine my presentations at rural clinics over the years. If I didn't survive this, I wanted Cilicia and the kids to at least have this evidence of my work among the people here.

"When you get to Kabul," I said, "hand this over to Roy."

Rafiq took the backpack, then removed his checkered head scarf and wrapped it around my neck. "Keep this so you stay warm," he said, his voice catching. "I am promising that we will come back for you."

Tears ran down my face as I gave him, and then Farzad, a long hug.

They walked about twenty feet to the edge of the plateau then turned. Rafiq motioned to his heart. Farzad touched his chest, then spread his palms. He was telling me to have a big heart.

"Yes, Farzad," I said. "Yes, I will do that."

They turned again and joined the Commander and his assistant. The Commander beckoned for the Urdu guy, who stood near me, to come over too. I motioned to the Urdu speaker, trying to convey "Can you stay?" If he remained with me, I might be able to communicate at least a little with these guys.

But my despair deepened when the Urdu speaker quickly turned away. Was he sorry about leaving me and couldn't look me in the eyes, or was he just eager to link up with the Commander and the others? Either way, I'd lost my last chance at talking with my captors.

In single file Rafiq, Farzad, and the others stepped onto the slope. In seconds they were out of sight.

Moments later the Butcher and Haqqani walked away from us and down a different side of the mountain. Suddenly there were just six of us left: Wallakah, Hopeless, Ahmed, Senior and Junior Mullah, and me.

I sat down in front of a large rock, put my head down, and sobbed. I'd never felt so alone.

I was stunned by what happened next.

Ahmed, the young wrestler who'd put me in a headlock two days before, walked over, crouched in front of me, and waited for me to raise my head. He looked into my reddened eyes. I saw no anger, hatred, or contempt in his expression. Instead, I detected compassion.

Slowly Ahmed pulled out part of the scarf that surrounded his head and neck and raised it toward my face. Then, to my astonishment, he ever-so-gently began to dry the tears on my cheeks.

I was so surprised that I didn't know what to do. A few seconds later he tapped his hand over his heart and, without a word, stood and walked away.

My sobs subsided a bit. Before I could recover from this amazing and unexpected display, however, Wallakah stepped into my view, crouched before me, and used his own scarf to carefully dry my tears. He also tapped his heart.

Incredibly, after Wallakah finished, Junior Mullah also took his place in front of me, removed the scarf that covered his face, and used it to wipe what remained of my tears. It later hit me that this was an especially vulnerable act by Junior Mullah since it was the first time he'd revealed his face.

I was blown away. These men were Taliban, kidnappers who associated with killers. In Wallakah's case, at least, he was a killer himself. They had abducted me and my friends in order to extort money to support a violent insurgency. Yet something in my plight had struck a chord in them and brought out the best that humanity has to offer.

We might not have been able to communicate in words, but the language of compassion is understood by all.

THE LAST NIGHT

CHAPTER SIXTEEN

3:30 P.M., SATURDAY

WALLAKAH WAVED HIS ARM AT ME, INVITING ME TO JOIN THE others as they sat in a circle at the top of the mountain. Still moved by what had just happened, I did not hesitate to take a spot next to my captors. For good or ill, my fate now rested in the hands of these men.

Rafiq and Farzad were gone, hopefully on their way to being released. I was on my own. My mind raced as I tried to think of solutions. If I could somehow convince these guys to let me go, I could keep in touch with them, hitchhike to Kabul, get some money from my family and friends to pay them. But how could I convince them to release me? It was a crazy idea, but I was feeling desperate.

Hopeless made a fire at the edge of our circle. The base of the big rock where Senior Mullah still sat served as a windshield. I watched, fascinated, as Hopeless then removed the cleaning rod from his Kalashnikov, produced a plastic bag with leftover meat from last night's dinner, and proceeded to mount pieces of the meat on the rod, using it as a skewer. He jammed a few sticks into the ground in front of the fire, creating a makeshift mount for the rod. In no time, we were being treated to barbecued lamb.

141

I was incredibly thirsty, but our group had no water. I repeatedly said, "*Pani*," the Hindi-Urdu word for water, and pointed to the side of the mountain we'd climbed up earlier, remembering the pool we'd encountered on the trail. Yet the answer was always "No *pani*." Apparently they didn't want to go back that way. They must have still been worried about being discovered by the other Taliban.

Senior Mullah eventually pulled another Fresh & Cool gum stick from his pocket and handed it to me. It did help me produce some saliva for a few minutes, but when I was done, it left me thirstier than before.

Once we finished eating, the Taliban began packing up. We gathered at the edge of the plateau and began our descent down the steep mountainside and toward the valley.

Wallakah was next to me. As soon as we started, he said, "Rafiq, Farzad—brothers." He pronounced it "buh-ruh-thers."

That simple statement meant a lot to me. One of my favorite Afghan proverbs said, "The first time we meet, we are friends. The next time we meet, we are brothers." Wallakah's words reminded me of this. He was acknowledging that my relationship with Rafiq and Farzad went beyond friendship. He seemed touched by the fact that a foreigner like me could love Afghan people, his people, as brothers.

Yet Wallakah also had business to attend to with me. He pulled out a scarf and wrapped it around my head like a turban. Then he took the scarf Rafiq had given me, which I had around my neck, and wrapped it around my face so that only my eyes showed. He also removed one of his ammunition belts and slung it over my shoulder.

"You—shh," he said. "You mujahideen. Mujahideen Chechnya."

I got the idea. If we met someone, he wanted me to stay quiet and pose as one of them, a "freedom fighter." The mujahideen part I could understand. But from Chechnya? My appearance wasn't anything close to Russian. Yet there was little point in trying to argue about it. I simply nodded. Later I realized he was thinking of mujahideen who traveled to other lands to fight for freedom. I was to pretend I had gone to battle in Chechnya.

I didn't know if I should feel encouraged or more afraid that I now looked like my captors. If there was a rescue attempt, would they know it was me?

It was just after this that I noticed Junior Mullah was still showing his face, his scarf now wrapped around only his head. After he'd joined the group, Rafiq had said to me, "I might actually know him, but I cannot be sure because I can't see his face." We guessed that he was trying to hide his identity from us or, at least, from Rafiq. In a way I was touched that Junior Mullah had allowed me to see him. He apparently wasn't afraid of being identified by me.

I was also touched by the solicitous way my captors treated me as we made our way down. Several times we had to jump from one rock to another. The others were quick to offer a hand or grab ahold of me to help me keep my balance. Even Hopeless put out his hand a couple of times and said something like "Steady" or "Slow."

After about an hour, with the sun starting to set, we reached the base of the mountain. About a thousand yards beyond it was a large one-story home I'd seen from the mountain's peak. From up there I'd noticed it had a single section nearest us, separated from at least two more connected sections by a long wall. Now, as we headed straight toward the house, it was clear that this was our destination.

As we neared that first section, I saw that it was probably a single room, constructed of the usual stone and mud. The long stone wall, six feet tall, blocked our view of the rest of the house. This wall ran perpendicular to the front of the first room and extended about twenty feet from the right side of the room's front face, the wall and the room forming an *L* shape around a roofless veranda. The ground here was a smooth layer of mud and rock.

Wallakah led us across the veranda and into the only entrance to this section of the house, at the corner formed by the *L*. As he went in the door-sized opening, he called out, "Woo! Woo!"

It was indeed one room, about fifteen by twenty feet. Cushions lay on the smooth dirt floor. Four ventilation holes, each about a foot square, served as windows in the long entrance wall. Another five holes were visible along the far wall.

Moments later a slender man in his thirties entered the room. He was about five feet seven inches and wore a dark *salwar kameez*. This man greeted Wallakah as if he knew him.

Wallakah introduced him to the rest of us. When my turn came, Wallakah said something like, "This is a mujahideen who fought in Chechnya." I put my hand over my heart and bowed slightly, the traditional Afghan greeting, and took a seat on the floor with the others. The ruse seemed to be successful. I doubted our host knew I was a hostage.

Hopeless, Ahmed, and Junior Mullah all stacked their Kalashnikovs in the far corner of the room, away from the opening. I dropped my ammunition belt there too. Senior Mullah didn't carry a gun. The night before, when the sounds of that single-engine plane had been so prevalent, everyone had a heightened sense of the need for security. Nearly all of them kept their rifles close at hand. On this day, however, we hadn't seen or heard the plane since early afternoon. Security now seemed much less of a concern among my captors.

The lone exception was Wallakah. He kept his AK-47 slung over his shoulder. I would dearly wish later that he'd followed the lead of his colleagues.

Just after I sat down, another man entered the room. The slender man introduced him as a mujahideen fighting in Pakistan. When I heard that, I was glad I'd been identified as having fought in Chechnya. If Wallakah had introduced me as also fighting in Pakistan, I would have been expected to converse at length with this stranger.

The new man looked almost like a character out of a movie. He was stocky and clean shaven, with close-cropped black hair. He wore an American-style military camouflage uniform. His eyes were ringed in black with what looked like eyeliner but what was probably *surma*, an ore that some rural Afghans ground into powder and applied around the eyes. It was thought to improve vision as well as ward off evil.

What most grabbed the attention of the Taliban, however, was the stranger's light brown combat boots. They were tall, sturdy looking, and practically new. I could tell the others were impressed with this man and, especially, with his footwear. As the evening wore on, I heard the word *boots* several times as they talked and stole glances at him.

By this point my mouth felt drier than the southern region's Registan Desert. When a kettle of water was passed around, I drank almost half of it. Water had never tasted so good.

A round of tea soon followed, which also helped quench my thirst. I couldn't follow the conversation around me, of course, so I stayed quiet and observed. After previous hikes I'd noticed Hopeless rubbing the bottom of his foot, apparently to relieve pain. Now he sat in the corner, again rubbing his foot. I saw it had a peculiar, ball-like shape, and I wondered if an accident had left his foot deformed.

With the sun nearly down, the room had rapidly grown dark. The slender man carried in a lit kerosene lamp and placed it on the ground near the entrance. Then he began bringing us dinner. Our meal was lamb, rice, and naan, all served by the man who lived here. Though I never saw other members of the household, someone in one of the other rooms must have been preparing our food.

The room had been warm enough when we entered, but now I noticed a chill from the openings in the walls. After we finished dinner, our host began carrying rocks into the room and using them to plug the ventilation holes. I couldn't help wondering if one of the bigger stones might fall on someone's head during the night. Considering all the dangers I'd survived so far, it would be ironic if I was seriously injured during my sleep by a poorly secured rock.

Our host passed out two heavy blankets to each of us, almost a luxury in these parts. He also took a blanket and, with Wallakah's help, draped it over a thin rope that was fastened above the entryway. The blanket was dark brown with thick, black horizontal lines running across it. They reminded me of a tiger's stripes.

As soon as Hopeless received his blankets, he retreated to a spot in the far corner of the room, near the Kalashnikovs, and lay down. Soon after, I thought I heard him snore.

The slender man, meanwhile, brought out a kettle and a tray with six or seven glasses on it in preparation for another round of tea. I was exhausted and full from dinner, however. I decided to follow the example Hopeless had set.

"Thank you, no, but thank you," I said, rejecting the tea that was offered to me a minute later. "I am really satisfied." I suddenly realized I'd responded in English, but neither our host nor his other guest showed any reaction. Perhaps they believed I was practicing my English.

"Thank you, thank you," Wallakah said, imitating my words and smiling, revealing his crooked teeth. I returned his smile. He'd done that before during the last few days. I could tell he wasn't making fun of me. He was just so gregarious, always talking. It was his way of practicing a little English himself while connecting with me.

While the others conversed and drank their tea in a circle, I spread one of my blankets on the dirt floor near Hopeless and prepared to sleep. Wallakah's friendliness was still on my mind. I had the fleeting thought that if I got out of this, I could give him my long johns. In this harsh land he could make better use of them than I.

Soon tea was over, and our host and his mujahideen guest left us. The others got on their knees for *namaz*. Senior Mullah led Wallakah, Ahmed, and Junior Mullah in the prayer chants.

I didn't join them. Instead, I lay down, using my two head scarves as my new pillow and pulling the second blanket over my body. I turned away from Hopeless and the assault rifles in the corner. I didn't want to look at them. Instead, I faced the others and adjusted my hood to avoid breathing in dust from the blanket. I was just too tired to do anything more. Since Hopeless was already sleeping, I didn't feel too bad about it.

As I watched the others pray, I wondered what had been going through Hopeless's head this evening. I'd seen the uncertainty on his face. Was he contemplating his suicide mission? Did he skip *namaz* because he was tired or because he no longer cared? He and I had something in common—both of us were facing the strong possibility that our lives were about to end.

All those years ago, when I was a boy watching a documentary, I'd been so impressed by the Japanese doctor who'd served the people in rural China and ultimately given his life for them. It had crystallized my thinking, become part of my philosophy, without me even realizing it. The concept resonated with my soul then and still did now: if you truly believe in something, you should have the courage to live it out—and if necessary, even die for it.

It was my faith that gave me the strength to say this. I had tried to live in a way that served others and was pleasing to God. On that first long hike after our capture, I had made peace with him. If he was deciding that my time on this earth was done, I could and would accept that. I was in his hands.

Yet I wasn't giving up on this life. Somehow, I thought, I needed to convince the Taliban that I was their friend, that I didn't mean any harm to them, that they should release me. I didn't agree with most of their choices or their violent lifestyle, but I could still choose to love and connect with them as human beings. But how would I communicate any of this to them?

How in the world am I going to convince them to spare my life?

I went to sleep with many questions and no answers, yet trusting God with whatever would happen next.

At nearly the same moment back home, Cilicia was in our kitchen, serving a second helping of Saturday morning pancakes to our children. Asha, Jaron, Tobi, and Eshaan in his high chair were all in pajamas and gathered around our long dark-maple table. The day before, Asha and Jaron had finished school for the year. Today was the start of their Christmas vacation, but their minds were on something else.

"Mama, how is Papa doing?" Jaron asked, syrup dripping from his chin.

"When is he coming home?" Tobi asked.

Cilicia, about to drop a pancake from the spatula in her hand onto Jaron's plate, paused. Her hand wavered.

"I don't know," she said quietly. "The government is trying to help Papa."

"What is the government trying to do?" Asha asked.

Cilicia turned the spatula over. The pancake fell gently onto Jaron's plate. "They're doing something," she said. "But we don't know the details. We just need to pray that everything goes smoothly."

She wasn't going to cry. She wasn't. She needed to be strong in front of the kids.

Please, God, Cilicia prayed silently.

Please do let it all go smoothly.

RESCUE

CHAPTER SEVENTEEN

CHAPTER SEVENTEEN

12:20 A.M., SUNDAY, DECEMBER 9

SOMETHING WOKE ME UP.

The room was pitch dark. I heard the faint snoring of Hopeless, about a foot away from me on the floor, and the steady breathing of my other captors. Otherwise, it was deadly still. It felt like the middle of the night.

My nose was running, so I reached into my pocket for the well-used handkerchief I'd been carrying around the last four days. In Afghan culture, blowing your nose is offensive. It's good manners to excuse yourself and find a private place for such behavior. Sometimes, of course, that isn't an option. I've been in the middle of a lecture on hygiene techniques to rural Afghans when my nose starts to run. When that happens, I turn my back so no one can see me make a quick wipe.

This time I quietly rubbed my nose with my handkerchief. I tried to move as little as possible so I wouldn't wake anyone.

The only problem was that now *I* was fully awake. For the next five minutes I listened to the peaceful sounds of the Taliban at rest. Once again I mentally ran through the desperate plan I was hatching.

All I needed to do was find a way to communicate with my captors, convince them to let me go, stop for food and water at small towns along the way to Kabul, make my way into the city, find a way to get some money, and then pass that on to my kidnappers.

Right. It wasn't much of a plan. But it was all I had.

My thoughts were interrupted by the noise of a dog barking, followed by the bleating of a pair of sheep. Apparently our host's livestock were restless.

I heard someone in the room stir. Senior Mullah said something and was answered by Wallakah. From the sound of their voices, I could tell they were near the room's entrance, probably lying just three or four feet from the opening. I was about ten feet from the entryway. The others still seemed to be asleep—Hopeless on my right, Junior Mullah on my left, and Ahmed by my feet.

Senior Mullah and Wallakah exchanged more whispered words. Then I realized that Wallakah was slipping under the blanket that covered the entrance and stepping outside. Was something going on?

I listened intently but heard nothing. Wallakah returned less than a minute later and had another quiet chat with Senior Mullah. Their voices were neutral. It seemed Wallakah was just being his usual diligent self and apparently hadn't seen or heard anything unusual. I thought I heard him settle down again to sleep.

For the next few minutes I also tried to fall asleep. I wondered what had gotten the animals excited. Probably just another animal. Or maybe the wind. I again listened to the night—nothing.

I might have started to doze. I wasn't fully asleep, but I wasn't alert either.

The last thing I expected was for the world to explode.

Crack!

The gunshot was incredibly loud.

My eyes opened wide, my adrenaline suddenly spiking.

Fast movements in the room. Narrow beams of green light shooting this way and that. Multiple unfamiliar voices.

"Everyone put your hands in the air!"

"Everybody stand up! Stand up!"

"Put your hands where we can see them!"

What's going on? Wait a second. These guys are speaking English. They must be troops here for me!

Both Hopeless, on my right, and Junior Mullah, on my left, rolled toward me and on top of me, covering my body. At nearly the same instant Wallakah scrambled over and sat on my feet. Only my head was exposed.

I was amazed. Wallakah, gun in hand, could easily have shot me as the Commander had instructed on Friday night. Instead, these guys were protecting me.

"Stand up!"

"Stand up *now*!"

The voices around me were loud, tense, insistent. It seemed everyone in the room was shouting, soldiers and Taliban alike. I didn't know if the Taliban understood the command to stand, if the soldiers were gesturing "up" or if they were grabbing each of my captors and forcing them to their feet. But all the Taliban, except for Hopeless, quickly stood, and Hopeless rolled back off of me. I suspect Wallakah dropped his weapon at this point.

"Is Dilip Joseph here? Dilip Joseph?"

I had to swallow to make my voice work. From the ground I said, "Yes, I'm right here."

Immediately one of the soldiers lay on top of me, covering me with his body. At the same moment another soldier standing near my leg shouted at Hopeless, "Are you good or bad? Good or bad?"

When Hopeless didn't reply, this soldier yelled to me, "Is anybody else with you? What about your two friends?" I could barely hear him over everyone's voices.

"They were taken away earlier," I said. "I have no idea where they are."

"So are the rest of these guys good or bad?" the soldier shouted.

Hopeless spoke up then. I didn't know if he understood the soldier's words and tried to reply in English or if he was saying something else, but what came out was "Goo! Goo! Goo!"

"No, he's bad," I said. "He's bad."

Are these guys going to be taken to prison? Will they be killed? I hope not.

"Are you hurt anywhere?" the soldier on top of me asked. "Are you ambulatory? Can you walk?"

"Yes, I'm fine," I said. "I can walk. I'm not hurting anywhere."

A strange, muffled noise filled the room: *Pop! Pop! Pop!*

Oh, man! Did Hopeless reach for his gun? My captors are being shot!

"Have you been fed enough?" the man on top of me asked. "Are you tired? Did they abuse you?"

Pop! Pop!

Ah, this isn't what I expected. I can't believe this is how it's ending.

"Did they abuse you?"

Pop! Pop!

Man, life is ending all around me.

"You're going to be okay," the same soldier said. "We're going to get you out of here."

The soldier got off of me and helped me to my feet. He and another soldier sandwiched me between their shoulders and moved me toward the exit.

"Wait, guys," I said. "Give me a second to find my shoes."

They stopped. I turned.

I sensed, more than actually saw, bodies on the floor as my gaze immediately went to the figure that still breathed. He sat in an almost fetal posture, knees up with arms wrapped tightly around them, his chin resting on one knee.

Wallakah.

We were just three feet apart. He appeared unhurt.

Our eyes locked.

When Wallakah and the others first abducted me, I was certain I was about to die. I couldn't believe it. I felt shocked and desperate. At the same time, though, I still felt hope for my future—if not in this life, then in the afterlife.

Now, in the eyes of the young man who was my kidnapper and who had also, in a strange way, become almost a friend, I saw many of the same emotions. Shock. Desperation. Disbelief that he might be about to die.

Sadly, however, I did not see hope.

I wanted so much to reach out to Wallakah, to give him a hug. But I did not want to disrespect the soldiers around me. I owed them my life. In that moment I didn't think they would understand.

I have regretted my inaction ever since.

The look between Wallakah and me felt like hours, but it couldn't have been more than a few seconds. I broke away and focused on the floor to search for my shoes. Between the darkness and my shock about what was happening, I had trouble finding them. Finally I slipped them on and was escorted through the opening. The blanket was gone.

Several soldiers were moving about on the veranda. All wore night-vision goggles and carried weapons. The two soldiers with me steered me toward the outside wall just outside the room. "Stand right there," one of them said in a respectful tone. "Don't move around too much. Wait right here."

This is amazing, I thought. *How did these guys figure this out and find me?* I couldn't believe it.

I heard a radio crackle and a voice say that a helicopter was twelve minutes away. A minute later, a soldier said, "We're going to have you stand inside the room again and wait for a little bit."

A shard of fear sliced through me.

"There were five of them and four guns between them," I said. "Did you guys get all the guns?"

"Yes," the soldier answered. "Everything's been taken care of."

He took my left arm and guided me back toward the room. "When we go in," he said, "don't look around."

I didn't. Not at first. The soldier escorted me to the corner directly across from the entrance. I stood facing that corner for about five minutes and tried to wrap my mind around what had just happened.

I was safe. I was free. It didn't seem real.

When the soldier came to retrieve me, curiosity took over. I took a quick peek at the room as we walked out. The first thing I saw was Senior Mullah's body on the ground, blood oozing out of him in a dark pool.

The second thing I saw was Wallakah. He also was on the ground, a pool of blood beside him. Clearly he was dead. Had he made a last, desperate attempt to grab his gun? Had he tried to escape?

It didn't matter now. They all were dead.

I felt an overwhelming wave of sadness. These guys had put themselves in this position, of course. They'd aligned with the Taliban and aided or participated in a kidnapping. If not for this rescue, it was likely I'd be the one lying on the ground beside a pool of blood.

But I'd shared life with these men over the last four days. In one of the lowest moments of my life, some had even showed me unexpected compassion. I'd connected with them—Wallakah in particular.

Not so long before, I'd thought of staying in touch with these guys. I'd hoped I could influence them, demonstrate another way of life, help them see there were other choices they could make. Whether it had been realistic or not, that dream was now shattered.

When I was escorted outside, one soldier stood directly in front of me while another was right behind me. Another group attended to a comrade lying on a gurney. The fallen soldier had bandages wrapped around his head. The soldier behind me was mumbling something under his breath.

"What are you doing?" asked the man ahead of me.

"Praying for Nic," the soldier in back of me said. "Praying that he'll be okay."

I realized that the injury to the soldier on the gurney was serious. I learned later that he was a U.S. Navy SEAL, chief special warfare operator, a recipient of the Bronze Star and Purple Heart. He had the dangerous assignment of being the first man to enter our room that night. Wallakah, lying on the floor, had had just enough time to raise his Kalashnikov and get off one shot.

The bullet struck the SEAL in the forehead.

For the second time in as many minutes, I felt a terrible heaviness. This man had just taken the lead in rescuing me. Here in front of me was the cost of his service. He was a hero, and now he was fighting for his life. This wasn't the movies. It was real.

The same two SEALs stayed right next to me, protecting me with their bodies. They escorted me to the side of the house and told me to cover my face, though I couldn't figure out why. A few minutes later a large military helicopter roared into view. It landed in the yard in front of us, its spinning rotors making a steady *bom-bom-bom-bom* sound and kicking up debris. What felt like thousands of little rocks began pelting my body. I pulled my hood tighter over my face and forehead, which had been partly exposed. Now I understood why the SEALs had asked me to cover my face.

We ran to and up a ramp in the back of the helicopter. "You can sit there," one SEAL yelled over the sound of the engine and rotors, pointing to a bench along the inside wall.

Moments later another group of SEALs appeared. They carried the gurney that held Nic. These men gently loaded him into the helicopter. In seconds we were airborne. The deadly scene below us quickly receded from view.

In the cramped quarters of the helicopter, I watched Nic's teammates pump air into his lungs as they tried to resuscitate him. I knew he wasn't doing well. I hoped and prayed he would live. I wanted to thank him personally for what he'd done. I had lived on the brink of death for days and now had seen it up close. I didn't want to see any more.

I leaned against the side of the helicopter and took a long, slow breath. Unbelievably, my ordeal was over. The helicopter flew on into the Afghan night, carrying me farther and farther away from a nightmare and back toward the world I knew and loved.

REBORN

1:30 A.M., SUNDAY, DECEMBER 9
AFGHANISTAN MILITARY BASE

WHEN OUR HELICOPTER LANDED AT A MILITARY AIR BASE, I was greeted warmly by Lieutenant Colonel Nathan Hansen of the U.S. Army and Technical Sergeant John Sprague of the U.S. Air Force, both in camouflage uniforms. They put their arms around me and helped me down the ramp.

"How are you doing?" Colonel Hansen asked. "Are you able to walk to the truck over there?"

"I'm totally fine, thank you," I said. At almost the same moment that I stepped off the helicopter, a team of SEALs rushed by with its wounded comrade and the gurney. "Can you please keep me up to date on the man who was hurt?" I asked, watching them leave. I was definitely worried about his condition.

"We'll definitely do that," Colonel Hansen said. We got into a military truck and sped away.

"Dr. Joseph, I want you to be aware of how this is going to work," the colonel said as another soldier drove. "Your reintegration process is going to take four to five months. You'll need to spend a few weeks with us. Then you'll have two or three weeks in a neutral setting. Then we'll need to track you with counseling and care for another two or three months when you're back in the States."

That sounded complicated to me. I just wanted to go home. Of course, I was still in shock and probably not in the best shape to decide what I needed right then.

"Colonel, I know you're intending all of this for my good," I said. "Given what I've been through these last four days, all I want is to get back to my family."

Colonel Hansen studied me for a moment. "Let's go through the first two or three days and assess the situation at that point," he said.

"That sounds fine to me."

I was escorted to a base medical clinic, where a doctor examined me. Other than some soreness in my side from the Butcher's rifle blow, I felt fine, and I was given a clean bill of health.

As I walked out of the medical clinic office, I caught a glimpse of myself in a mirror. At least, I thought it was me. The dirty, hairy image reflected back looked more like a yeti than anyone I recognized.

The colonel and sergeant walked me across the base. "Has anyone contacted my family?" I asked.

"Your safe return has already been communicated," the colonel said. "You will definitely have the chance to call them after we get you to your room and you get a little rest."

I didn't protest. I realize now I was a bit disoriented. I really couldn't believe it was all over.

The two officers took me to a cabin, where two sergeants stood guard. Inside were three small rooms. My hosts showed me one of the rooms. It was basic soldier's quarters, with a bunk bed, desk, and closet.

To me, it looked like luxury. "This is yours for you to just rest," the colonel said. "If you need anything—food, drink, TV—just ask a sergeant."

I wasn't ready to rest yet, though. After five days of wearing the same outfit and sleeping on dirt, I wanted a long, hot shower and a change of clothes. One of the sergeants walked me to a large bathroom that had been locked and set aside just for me.

For the first time since I'd been abducted, I was truly alone. It was a strange feeling. I approached the mirror over the sink and examined myself.

Wow! I thought. *I look terrible.*

My face was covered with dust. My hair stuck out at crazy angles. I had a scraggly beard. My eyes had dark rings around them. It was hard to believe I'd been in captivity for only four days. Based on my appearance, you'd have thought it was four months.

More disturbing was the reflected image of my *salwar kameez*. I still recognized a few of the pomegranate stains from my meal at the police chief's house in Pul-i-assim on Wednesday, which seemed a lifetime ago. But much of these were covered by another dark-red substance. I had been splattered with blood.

It was a relief to take off those clothes and step into the shower. The water was cleansing in more ways than one. I felt as if I were scraping away a terrible burden that had attached itself to my body. All the worry and tension and fear that had clung to me for the past few days mixed with the soap and water on the shower floor and washed down the drain.

It felt so good.

By the time I'd changed into a fresh T-shirt, sweatpants, and military jacket provided by my new hosts, I felt at least a bit more like my old self. Back at my cabin I tried to rest on the bed. But my mind wouldn't relax.

What, I wondered, *do I do now? Will they let me call Cilicia and the kids? What about my sister, my uncle, my dad? Are Rafiq and Farzad safe? What's next?*

At about four thirty, Colonel Hansen and Sergeant Sprague returned to the cabin and said I was welcome to call my family if I was ready to do that. Of course I was ready! They advised me to keep this first call brief.

I soon understood why. Alone in my room, phone in hand, I waited for what seemed an eternity for the connection to go through to Colorado Springs. It was five in the afternoon on Saturday there.

"Hello?" It was Cilicia's voice.

"Hi, honey. It's me. I just want you to know . . . that I'm okay."

That was all either of us could manage. We both started crying.

It didn't matter. Words weren't important at that point. Just hearing each other's voices and connecting again—knowing that we would see each other again—was all we needed.

I called my sister, also keeping that call short to give her a chance to recover from the emotional roller coaster she'd been through. She said she would contact my father, who'd been traveling and had only heard about the kidnapping the day before. Then I connected with Roy, who passed on the wonderful news that Rafiq and Farzad were both well and out of harm's way.

It was only later that I heard the details of the amazing story of Rafiq and Farzad's journey to safety. Both tribal influence and the efforts of family played important roles in their survival.

Rafiq was part of the Khugiani tribe, born and raised in an area called the White Mountains, not far from where we had all hiked. When his extended family, including six uncles, nephews, and other close relatives, heard about the kidnapping—as did members of the villages where Rafiq worked—all were outraged. They learned who some of the kidnappers were and went to their family homes, demanding our release. Some found out who was behind the abduction and called the Commander directly to insist that we be freed. Though I didn't know it at the time, I had witnessed some of these calls.

It turned out that the Taliban had lied to us about the Hilux full of armed men. They weren't Taliban from Pakistan trying to take us away, but members of Rafiq's family intending to liberate us. When I heard this, I finally understood why our captors had been in such a hurry to get away.

The last time I'd seen my friends, they were hiking down the mountain with the Commander, his assistant, and the black-outfitted Urdu guy. Rafiq's legs stiffened, and he had trouble keeping up with the others. He fell to the end of the line, though one of the Taliban stayed within visual range.

After they were off the mountain, another man suddenly appeared on the trail and ran toward Rafiq. He recognized Rafiq from his work in the villages. "Who are these men you're with?" the man asked. "What is happening here?"

Rafiq had been told by the Taliban to say nothing. Fearing for his life, he said, "I cannot answer you." The man ran off.

Rafiq eventually caught up with the other Taliban. They'd been joined by at least two other Taliban from Pakistan. When they rounded a bend in the trail, they were opposed by a group of about ten villagers. The villagers had been alerted by the man on the trail and were angry.

"We hear in the news that three doctors were kidnapped," one villager said. "Where is the other? You want to kill them, sell them? What is your plan?"

"No, that's wrong," the Commander said. He made up a story about helping these two "shepherds" look for their lost animals.

An argument ensued. More villagers kept arriving. Some carried stones. Soon the crowd swelled to as many as seventy people.

The Commander tried to lead Rafiq, Farzad, and the rest of the group past the villagers. They made it about a hundred yards before they were stopped again. This time, pushing and shoving led to a fight between the villagers and the Taliban. The Taliban didn't raise their guns, perhaps because there were too many villagers to subdue. The fight broke up after a few minutes. No one was seriously injured, though someone smashed the glasses of an older Talib from Pakistan.

The Taliban managed to take Rafiq and Farzad to a house, though they were still under the watchful eyes of some of the villagers. After tea Rafiq and Farzad were escorted by six armed Taliban, including the Commander and his assistant, to a remote location. There they met Farzad's brother and cousin, who'd driven there in a car. Their arrival was supposedly part of Rafiq's plan to bring money to the Taliban in exchange for their release.

What the Taliban didn't know was that Rafiq's family had also alerted Afghanistan's military and intelligence network.

The Taliban pushed Rafiq and Farzad into the backseat of the vehicle; then the Commander and his assistant also climbed in, one on each side of Rafiq and Farzad. Both carried AK-47s. With the brother driving and the cousin in the front passenger seat, the six of them drove off. The two Taliban expected that they were about to get their money.

What happened instead was that after driving a few minutes on a dirt road, they reached pavement. And a minute after that, they came to a checkpoint manned by Afghan National Security Forces.

Uniformed men quickly surrounded the car, weapons raised. There was nothing the two Taliban could do.

One of the security men saw Rafiq and smiled. "Rafiq, we found you," he said. "Be happy." For Rafiq and Farzad, it was a moment of overwhelming relief.

Reborn, Rafiq told himself. *I am reborn.*

At the base, I spent the rest of my first morning as a free man in debriefing meetings. I related my experience to the colonel and sergeant, to representatives of the U.S. Embassy, and to the FBI, first in separate meetings and then later to groups that combined members from different agencies. The repetition was actually beneficial—it was healing for me to get the story out. I also met with a chaplain and his assistant.

I learned that an embassy official named Rahim had been involved in my rescue and coordinated much of the service I was now enjoying. He was in charge of crisis citizen services for the state department. I thought his work was an amazing example of our increasingly multicultural world. A Muslim South Asian–American had helped retrieve a Christian Indian-American being held by Muslim extremists in Afghanistan. I'd always admired America for being a place where people of different cultures and beliefs could exist and thrive side by side. Now I was seeing firsthand another example. Though I'd lived in many countries, I'd yet to experience this anywhere else in the world.

"Dr. Joseph," Rahim said, "I want you to know that for the past forty-eight hours, you were at the top of the U.S. government's priority list. That included President Obama and all the way down the line."

I was truly humbled to hear this.

When I walked back to my cabin after my debriefing meetings, I met yet another officer who'd played a key role in securing my freedom. Standing next to my door was an air force captain.

When I was close enough, I checked his nametag: David Norse.

"Norse," I said. "I know that name." I remembered an air force officer named Norse who'd made an off-site video presentation right after mine for a leadership seminar.

I eventually learned that Captain Norse had taken part in planning and coordinating my rescue, which included the Navy SEAL team and air force pararescue and combat control special operators. He also was in charge of my reintegration process at the base and coordinated my meetings with the different agencies.

I was amazed. The army of people who'd been part of my liberation seemed to keep growing.

Throughout my meetings the status of the wounded SEAL continued to weigh on my mind. I'd repeatedly asked Colonel Hansen, "How is the man doing who got shot?" He wouldn't tell me, which I knew couldn't be good. Finally, early that afternoon, he was cleared to fill me in.

"Dilip, I'm very sorry to inform you that the operator who went in first during the rescue essentially gave his life for you. He passed away."

I wasn't surprised to hear it, but it still hit me hard. This man, someone I'd never even met, had made the ultimate sacrifice for me. How could I process this? What had I done to deserve an act as selfless as this? What would his death mean for his family, his friends? Once again I was humbled beyond words.

U.S. Navy SEAL operators—SEAL stood for Sea, Air, and Land— are the secretive men who take on the military's most dangerous missions. Their training is so rigorous that class dropout rates sometimes exceed 90 percent. They have been active in Afghanistan since shortly after 9/11 and have rescued a number of Americans at risk around the world. These include Captain Richard Phillips, from a group of Somali pirates in 2009, and aid worker Jessica Buchanan, from Somali terrorists in 2012, as well as a boatload of raids that no one has ever heard about.

I found out that the men involved in my rescue were part of the same team that had participated in the most famous SEAL operation of all—the May 2011 raid on a compound in Abbottabad, Pakistan, that resulted in the death of Osama bin Laden. They were members of the U.S. Naval Special Warfare Development Group, more commonly known as SEAL Team Six.

Colonel Hansen told me that the SEALs would be honoring Nic that night with a special "ramp ceremony," the traditional SEAL memorial service for a fallen fellow warrior. When I heard this, I saw an opportunity.

"Colonel, is there any chance I could attend the ceremony?" I asked. "If the whole rescue team is going to be there, could I have a chance to thank them?"

The colonel promised to see what he could do, though he made it clear that getting clearance would be difficult. Later that day, however, he returned with good news: "Dilip, after getting to know you over these past few hours, I felt I could speak firmly of your character. We've made sure you'll have the opportunity to attend the ceremony and speak to the SEALs tonight. It will be good for the team and just as good for you. I think it will start the process of your healing."

I was so glad to hear the colonel say this. But as the evening wore on, I grew increasingly nervous about it. What would I say to these guys? What did they think of me? Were they glad they'd taken part in my rescue, or did they view me as the guy who'd caused their friend to die?

More than once during the day, Colonel Hansen had encouraged me by saying, "You have been rescued, and you have returned with honor." I thought it was his way of conveying that I shouldn't feel shame or survivor's guilt. I wasn't sure if I agreed with those ideas or not, but his words meant a lot to me.

Finally, just after midnight on what was now Monday morning, I joined the SEALs and other officers on the airfield tarmac. I felt out of place, like a dolphin in the middle of a desert.

As people milled about and waited for the ceremony to begin, the SEAL shoot commander walked up and greeted me. "I hear you want to say something to my boys," he said. "They rarely have the chance to hear a word of thanks from anyone. So whatever you want to say, make it count."

I was nervous before. Now I definitely felt the pressure.

The SEAL senior commander also greeted me, saying it was an honor to be part of my rescue. Then he walked over to another officer and tapped him on the shoulder. This man, in a camouflage uniform and hat, broke away from his conversation and came to shake my hand.

"Dr. Joseph, my name is General Allen," he said. "I just want you to know that we're so glad you're safely back with us."

I'd already realized that the rescue mission had touched the highest levels of the U.S. government. Now I had even more evidence of it. General John Allen was the commander of all ISAF troops and additional U.S. forces in Afghanistan.

Just before the ceremony began, Colonel Hansen rejoined me. I think he sensed my anxiety.

"Don't worry so much about the words you're going to use," he said. "Just speak from your heart. Just thank them. That's all you have to do."

Once again I appreciated the colonel's encouragement and insight. It came just in time.

The ceremony began with the arrival of Nic's casket. The casket was draped with an American flag. More than one hundred military personnel lined up at attention and saluted as eight pallbearers slowly and silently carried the casket up a ramp and into the back of an enormous cargo plane, a Boeing C-17.

Nic's SEAL teammates joined him inside the C-17 to pay their final respects while the rest of us waited below.

When the ceremony ended, Colonel Hansen asked me to walk up the ramp and speak. Once inside the giant metal tube, I saw that the casket had been moved to the far end of the plane's interior. While I stood with my back to the opening at the tail, nearly thirty SEALs gathered in front of me in a semicircle.

"As a medical doctor," I began, "I can appreciate what it means to save lives. But what you guys did for me last night—"

My eyes began to well with tears. My voice broke so that I could barely get the words out. I hoped they could understand me.

"What you guys did for me," I continued, "goes way beyond even my imagination. The courage and commitment and strength that you've shown to rescue me from my situation speak volumes. To do that at the cost of sacrificing one of your own means so much to me."

U.S. Navy SEALs have a reputation as the toughest people on the planet, one they have rightly earned from their training and from the skill they've demonstrated in mission after mission. But as I observed the faces of the men gathered around me, I saw more than a few eyes, like mine, filling up. A few of the SEALs had tears running down their cheeks.

As I finished, my voice was nearly inaudible. "Your service and sacrifice will not be forgotten," I said. "The memory of what you did for me will live on in our family for generations to come."

When I finished, the SEALs lined up in single file. Not one left the plane until he'd shaken my hand. I had the opportunity to look into the eyes of each man and thank him for what he'd done. Their responses varied. Some said, "It was our pleasure," or "It was an honor to serve you." Others simply replied, "You're welcome" or said nothing at all.

It didn't really matter. I wasn't looking for a response. I just wanted to personally express my gratitude to these American heroes, men who tackle the toughest assignments, always dangerous and never in the limelight.

They had given me my life back and allowed me to share in a private memorial to one of their finest. The chance to have a moment with each of them was meaningful beyond measure. It is carved permanently into my life story, part of a night I will never forget.

After all the SEALs had walked down the ramp, Colonel Hansen clapped me on the back. "What you had to say out there really encouraged those guys," he said. "You did well."

I remained on the plane for another minute to regain my composure. When I walked down to the tarmac, I was surprised to see that all the SEALs were still there, waiting for me. They wanted a group picture. Once that was done, the team leader again shook my hand.

"We can tell that the type of work you do is quite commendable and very important to you," he said. "It probably makes a huge difference in the lives that you serve. It's obvious you really love what you do. It's been an honor to serve you.

"But," he added, "if you ever come back to Afghanistan, we will kill you."

The team leader half smiled as he said this. I knew it was a joke, of course. But at the same time I understood that it also wasn't. He was reminding me of all that had transpired to bring me here.

He then handed me what I first thought was a large gold coin. "We would like you to have this," he said, "as a token of our service to you."

After he left, I took a closer look. The coin was actually shaped like a shield. It featured the SEAL symbol, which included a trident, pistol, and eagle, signifying the SEAL's abilities at sea, on land, and in the air. This symbol was overlaid on a huge Roman numeral VI.

The colonel explained that it was a rare SEAL Team Six medallion. "You should know that only a handful of people in the world have that medallion," the colonel said. "Do not sell that on eBay."

I laughed. "I wouldn't do that," I said. "Believe me; this is something I will always cherish."

Back at my cabin I reflected on the incredible events of the last few hours. I was exhausted, both physically and emotionally drained. Yet in a strange way I also felt uplifted. In addition to fear and desperation, I'd also experienced moments of unexpected humanity during my days with my Taliban kidnappers. Despite the horrible circumstances I'd discovered a new hope.

Now here, among the best and bravest of America's military, I'd experienced that humanity and hope once again. I felt privileged to be alive and in the presence of these dedicated men. Everything I accomplished in life from this point forward would be possible only because of them.

Like Rafiq and Farzad, I, too, had been reborn.

I crawled into bed—a real bed with sheets and blankets, provided and protected by the U.S. military even in this far corner of the world—and put my head on the pillow. A few minutes later I fell into a deep and restful sleep.

HOME

CHAPTER NINETEEN

5:30 P.M., MONDAY, DECEMBER 10

MY MONDAY WAS FILLED WITH MORE MEETINGS. THIS TIME REP-
resentatives from the FBI and U.S. Embassy repeated my story back
to me to make sure they had the facts correct. I also participated in
an hour-long call with a public relations official in Washington, D.C.,
who advised me on what to say in a press release and how to deal with
the media. He let me know that I'd exhaust myself if I tried to talk
with everyone. That was helpful to remember when the media requests
began pouring in on my return to the States.

I also met again with the base chaplain and his assistant. They were
especially excited about hearing what was going on in the country beyond
the city of Kabul and the base. I told them that contrary to what many
believed, the rural people had many dreams and aspirations—hopes of
advancing their education, securing better jobs, and seeing their children
grow up with more freedoms and opportunities.

Early in the afternoon, an embassy official pulled me aside. "Dr.
Joseph," he said quietly, "we are picking up intelligence that your life
may still be in danger. So we're moving you tonight to the U.S. Embassy
in Kabul."

The official didn't explain further, but I wasn't too worried. After all I'd been through, this seemed more an inconvenience than anything else. I trusted that I was in good hands.

Now I was on the base airfield, back in a military helicopter. We lifted into the twilight for the second helicopter ride of my life. Colonel Hansen and four other officials accompanied me. We flew to Kabul International Airport, where a convoy of SUVs transported me to the embassy. Two men joined us in the SUV. They wore suits and carried automatic weapons. One of them handed a weapon to the colonel and gave him a security briefing.

I might not have been worried, but clearly these guys took their jobs seriously.

I spent the night at the embassy. The original U.S. Department of Foreign Affairs, I learned, was established and signed into law in 1789 by President George Washington. One of its early purposes was to help protect U.S. civilians from pirate attacks.

Not long after we arrived, Rahim apologized to me. I'd requested a meeting with Rafiq, Farzad, Roy, and other members of our NGO's team in Kabul. I wanted to see again the friends I'd shared my ordeal with, as well as thank the friends and colleagues who had done so much to help secure my release. Rahim told me, however, that for security reasons they'd had to cancel our appointment. Because of the security risk and because I seemed to be recovering quickly, they had decided to fly me out of the country in the morning.

I was deeply disappointed to miss what would have been an emotional and heartwarming reunion. Either over the phone or in person, these were the people who had shared and encouraged me through the most harrowing days of my life. I felt more connected to them now than ever and so wanted that time to gain a sense of closure.

Despite this letdown, I more than welcomed the rest of the embassy official's news. I was going home.

At five thirty the next morning, I heard a knock on the door to my room. Standing there was a familiar and smiling face—Jerry, a fellow doctor from Chicago who worked at the CURE International Hospital in Kabul. Morning Star and the embassy staff had arranged for him to fly back home with me.

"Hey, Dilip, how are you doing?" Jerry said while giving me a hug.

I laughed. "I'm doing okay, Jerry. Glad you could come along."

I felt better already. After so much intensity, Jerry's friendly and easygoing nature was just what I needed.

Later that morning I traveled with Jerry, Colonel Hansen, Rahim, and Jay, another embassy staff member, to the Kabul airport. I carried with me reminders of my captivity—the piece of naan, the gum wrapper, one remaining piece of cloth—as well as important mementos from my time at the base and embassy. In addition to a new passport and some cash, Rahim gave me a gold-plated coin representing the U.S. Embassy. It featured an eagle holding an olive branch in one talon and a group of arrows in the other. I put the coin in my bag with the SEAL medallion.

I also carried the military Bible that was provided for me in my cabin at the base. Most of the officers I'd come to know and respect in the last two days had signed it. One of them was Jay, the embassy worker who was also an ex-SEAL and had played an important part in coordinating my rescue. He had signed my Bible with a verse from the book of Isaiah, which reads, "Then I heard the voice of the Lord saying, 'Whom shall I send? And who will go for us?' And I said, 'Here am I. Send me!'"[1] It had helped inspire him to join the military so he could serve others.

So many of the people I'd met since early Sunday morning had, like Jay, demonstrated amazing passion for their work—for taking care of civilians like me, for serving their country with honor, for doing the job right. It made me proud to be an American.

While we sat and waited for the plane, Rahim received a text that made him smile. It was from the secretary for the U.S. ambassador to Afghanistan. The ambassador had planned to meet with me later that day, but my top-secret departure had changed the plan.

"You can tell your NGO friends that they shouldn't feel too bad about not meeting you," Rahim said. "Even the U.S. ambassador won't have the chance to meet you."

Soon I was shaking hands and saying good-bye to Colonel Hansen, Rahim, and Jay. I would never be able to thank them enough for what they'd done. Then Jerry and I boarded the military contractor plane. After a half-day layover in Dubai and a thirteen-hour commercial flight, we landed on U.S. soil in Washington, D.C. on what was Wednesday morning in America.

Throughout my trip I'd had the feeling I was being watched. It seemed as if every time I turned around, men in dark suits and sunglasses were nearby, observing while pretending not to observe.

I figured it was more than just my imagination when Jerry and I were met by a team of FBI agents once we walked off the jet bridge and into the Dulles International terminal. Among the agents was Mary, the woman who had been extremely helpful and comforting over the phone to both Cilicia and Deepa. Mary wanted me to appreciate what had happened. "Your case is unique," she said. "Few people get out of situations like yours." The agents then explained the services the FBI would provide for me now that I was in the States.

A few hours later we landed in Los Angeles and met another group of agents. My sister, Deepa, greeted me with a long, powerful hug and a relieved smile. We spent the night and morning with Deepa and her family, then took off the next day for Colorado Springs.

When our plane landed, FBI agents escorted me to a side exit. I suddenly realized Jerry was no longer with me and asked what had happened.

"He's getting off with the other passengers," one agent said. "Don't worry. Jerry's well taken care of."

I was sorry I didn't even get the chance to say good-bye to my friend. But I didn't have much time for regret. There at the bottom of the mobile stairs was Daniel.

"Dilip, I'm so glad to see you," he said after a hug.

"I'm very glad to be home."

More FBI agents ushered me into an SUV. They drove me to a retreat center in the Colorado Springs area. I would spend the next three nights there, secluded from the media and other responsibilities and at last allowed the chance to unwind after all I had been through.

The moment I'd hoped for, waited for, and prayed for almost since I'd been abducted finally arrived. It was already dark when I reached a log cabin with three or four units inside. I climbed the steps of the porch and pushed on the heavy wood door that led into a hallway.

The door swung open, and there was Cilicia, holding little Eshaan, standing up and waiting for me.

Just as in that first phone call, words were unimportant. I managed to say, "Honey, how are you?" That was about it. We hugged and just held each other. When you're living out a miracle, you don't need to make a big speech. You just take it in with gratitude.

That time at the retreat center was wonderful. I couldn't believe how much Eshaan had grown since I'd last seen him nearly a month before. A fresh helping of joy filled my heart at the thought that I would get to know him better and watch him grow after all.

The other three kids were with my sister-in-law. We got the entire family back together for the first time on Saturday and then went home on Sunday.

Now that I was back in familiar surroundings, it almost seemed as if nothing had changed. I knew that wasn't true, though, when Asha asked, "Papa, do you know how famous you are now? You're on TV all the time," and when Tobi kept using the latest word he'd added to his vocabulary: *captured*.

When the kids' bedtime arrived on our first evening back home, we helped them into their pajamas and gathered in the living room for our usual good-night prayers. When I sat on the couch, Cilicia held Eshaan while the three oldest kids fought for position and tried to snuggle with me.

It seemed they'd missed having Papa around. I'd missed them too.

I closed my eyes. "Dear God," I said, "thank you for bringing me home safely and for putting the right people in place and orchestrating events so that I could be rescued. Thank you for allowing me to return to my family. Thank you for your blessings. We pray that you would be with each of us tonight, tomorrow, and in the days and years ahead. Amen."

I opened my eyes and exchanged smiles with Cilicia. I had survived the worst ordeal of my life with my faith and hope intact. God had been there throughout my captivity and would be there still. He had given me a new chance at life.

I intended to cherish every moment of it.

HEARTACHE AND JOY

May 2014
Colorado Springs, Colorado
WHEN I RETURNED HOME FROM AFGHANISTAN A YEAR AND A half ago, I had no intention of writing a book about my experience. Yet when I described the events of my kidnapping and rescue to others, they invariably told me in one way or another, "This is amazing and important. People need to hear about this. You need to tell your story." Their continuing encouragement led to what you've just read.

I have been blessed, not only by my rescue but also by how I've been able to deal with the impact of my ordeal. In those first two weeks back in the States, I had trouble falling asleep as I replayed events and realized how easily things could have turned out differently. I also had a couple of nightmares. Once, I woke up thinking I'd been shot.

Since then, however, I've worked through much of the trauma from my captivity. I've seen no signs of post-traumatic stress disorder. I attribute much of this to the excellent care and counseling that began as soon as I reached the military base in Afghanistan and continued after I returned home. This, combined with my strong belief that God is in control of my life and will bring good out of all my experiences, even a kidnapping, has made for a relatively smooth transition back to my normal life.

The transition hasn't been as smooth for my two friends and colleagues, Rafiq and Farzad. Unlike here in the West, their culture does not promote the same level of social and professional care that I received after my release. And unlike me, they could not leave it all behind when they went back to their families. For them, home remains a dangerous place, the fear of Taliban reprisal very real. In fact, both they and their families left Afghanistan for four months in 2013 because the risk of staying in the area was so high.

Yet now they are back. Dangerous or not, Afghanistan is their home. Rafiq has told me that he still has a great passion to help his people, to give them new opportunities in medicine, education, and building a greater sense of community. He refuses to live in fear. Every day I admire the strength and courage of my two friends and pray for their safety.

None of this has been easy for my wife or extended family as well. It's been healing for me to talk and write about what I went through. Everyone is different, however. For Cilicia and my extended family, answering questions about those days and reliving the experience brings back all the stress and worry. I'm so sorry about all they've had to endure.

Afghanistan continues to be a challenging place to work. The Taliban remain active, and innocent lives continue to be lost. One loss in particular weighs heavily on my mind. I will never forget the sacrifice of a brave twenty-eight-year-old. He served his country with honor and was decorated many times over. He was a Pennsylvanian who, even as a youth, wanted to serve his country as a Navy SEAL. He was a born leader who loved life and brought joy to everyone around him. The shoot commander at the base said he was "one of my best." By the way he said it, I knew he meant every word. Because of Nic's courage and that of his teammates, my children still have their papa. His service is a debt I can never repay.

And then there are my Taliban captors, in particular Wallakah. Yes, I grieve for them, too, though perhaps not in the same way as others. That may be hard to understand. To me, every life on this planet is precious. I am a doctor. My passion is to bring holistic healing—physical, emotional, mental, and spiritual—to everyone. Of course, I realize that Wallakah, Hopeless, Ahmed, and Senior and Junior Mullah were part of the group that kidnapped and threatened me. During their lives, they made terrible and even evil decisions. But who can say what I would have done if I'd grown up in their shoes? After connecting with Wallakah and some of the others and seeing their humanity, I can't help feeling sad about their loss. There was potential, at least, for change and a better future.

That said, I certainly have nothing but respect and admiration for the SEALs and their actions. They entered a hostile situation to save me and were fired upon by my captors. They also had to be concerned about the possibility that one or more of the Taliban wore a suicide vest or had another hidden weapon, or that other Taliban might arrive on the scene. I will always be grateful that these brave Americans risked their lives for mine.

After so much violence and death, the question continues to be raised: Is it worth it for me and others to continue to put our lives at risk in Afghanistan? From my point of view, the answer is unquestionably yes.

Some would argue this from a strategic and security perspective, saying that even a limited U.S. military presence in the country will continue to help prevent al-Qaeda and other terrorist groups from training jihadists and launching attacks against our homeland. This is likely true, but it's not the main motivation behind my answer.

Though it's not often reported in the media, Afghanistan has come a long way since the rule of the Taliban. Government-sanctioned public executions are part of the past. Women, admittedly in small numbers, hold jobs and even positions in parliament. Roughly seven million of the twelve million eligible voters in Afghanistan braved nasty weather and threats of Taliban violence to vote in the April 2014 presidential election. That's a higher percentage than we often see in the United States.

Most Afghans in the cities, especially the youth, welcome help from America and other outside entities. They have seen how opportunities for education and an improved economy can change their lives for the better.

I have personally observed this openness to foreigners. Every time I go to Afghanistan, visiting villagers see what our NGO staff is doing with medical clinics and education programs and ask us to open community centers in their own villages. We always have to say no because of our limited resources. I remember one young man in particular who said, "You guys are doing such a great job here. Please do this work in my village too. If no one makes this kind of effort, most of us will end up joining the Taliban."

Community development in a nation such as Afghanistan is certainly a challenge. The idea is to start a program that will eventually stand on its own. Yet there are so few local resources, and often so little hope among the people, that getting to that point takes a long-term commitment. We *are* making steady progress. The advances in medical care and education are paralleled by new relationships among the rural people. Leaders of different tribes, as well as women from different villages, are talking to one another for the first time, leading to greater collaboration and understanding.

I do have hope for Afghanistan's future. My hope lies especially in what I see in this nation's young people. I remember Ajmal, the teen who spoke so eloquently at the debate tournament in Kabul just a few days before my kidnapping. He exuded enthusiasm, passion, and leadership potential. These were the same qualities I was soon to observe in another young man of nearly the same age: Wallakah. They came from different backgrounds but had much in common.

And what about the Taliban, you ask. Is there any hope that these violent fundamentalists might one day lay down their arms and join the majority of the nation in seeking a more peaceful and cooperative future?

Again I say yes—under certain conditions. A continuing commitment to community development is vital. It will take people showing the Taliban that another way of life is possible and beneficial, that they can live and thrive by joining with others rather than excluding. It will also take village elders with the courage to say, "This is not working. We're not going to live this way anymore." The Taliban cannot exist as an organization without the support of villagers.

Then there is the matter of faith. The Taliban are driven by self-righteousness. They believe that God wants them to kill in order to purify their tribe and nation. This includes both infidels and their own people if they oppose Taliban views. The Taliban want to separate themselves from the rest of the world. Yet the Koran also teaches Muslims to respect their fellow human beings. If only the Taliban would embrace what they accept in theory but so rarely put into practice—that the world belongs to God and that he loves all his people.

As I have gone through the different stages of life, I have learned the value of assessing my spiritual growth. While my journey is at times challenging, it is a worthy one. For me, it is less about being religious and adhering to rules and routines and more about seeing and caring for others through the loving eyes of God. I try to rely always on God's grace and mercy, to understand his ways in my life, and to project his love to others.

I am not so naïve as to suggest that achieving dramatic changes among the Taliban will be easy. Not at all. It will be a long, difficult struggle filled with setbacks. But I believe it is both possible and worth the effort. The Taliban are known for having closed minds, yet this is not what I experienced while talking with Wallakah, Haqqani, and some of the others. They realized they were at a dead end and sought something different. Thousands of people in Afghanistan—city dwellers and villagers and Taliban alike—are hungry for a better life. They are searching for answers if only someone will show them the way.

Will I be one of those people? As I write this, I don't know. My son Jaron was probably four years old when he said to me, "You know, Papa, I know why you go to Afghanistan. People really need your help." They still need my help today. My passion to continue my work among people I've grown to love is as strong as ever.

Many of us are quick to recognize measurable progress in developing nations—higher percentages of healthy babies, lower death rates among mothers during childbirth, decreasing reports of disease. But so much of what we do cannot be charted on a graph. As I've worked in Afghanistan and interacted with its people, I have experienced so much hope, joy, and peace. Simply taking the time to talk and listen with respect has an amazing impact. It is measured not in numbers but in smiles, trust, and new relationships. When we invest in those who are vulnerable and disenfranchised, our lives become more fulfilling.

I long to renew this work and had actually planned to return to Afghanistan for the first time in March 2014. But my passport mysteriously disappeared after I mailed it to the Afghanistan Embassy in Washington, D.C. Since then I've endured the deaths of friends, gained a better understanding of the emotional toll of such a trip on my family, and heard repeated advice from new friends in the military to stay away for now. While I continue to pray about the timing of my return, I will pursue creative ways to make a difference, even from a distance. After all, lasting change does not depend only on me. It was the combined efforts of many that allowed me to make a positive difference on previous trips. It will take more of this kind of team effort by both the Afghan people and the international community to keep the country moving forward.

As I think about Afghanistan and my own future, I realize that life is more precious to me than ever. I am reminded of this every time I look at my wife—at the time of this writing, we are expecting our fifth child. The joy my family brings me continues to outweigh the trials and heartaches.

If I have learned anything from my abduction and rescue, it is that God is in complete control of my life, regardless of what happens to me. I knew that before, but now it is branded indelibly in my psyche. I also understand that he loves me and that I can trust him.

When I was six years old, I had an experience that deepened this love and trust. I was in bed in my pajamas when my mother sat down and gently told me we could not afford the spoonful of sugar she usually added to my milk each night. "But I am going to pray that God would sweeten this milk for you, Dilip," she said, "and that as you drink, it would be the best milk you've ever had."

Even at that age, I was skeptical of my mother's words. How, I thought, was this going to work?

But sure enough, when I drank, it really was one of the best and sweetest glasses of milk I'd ever tasted. I was so amazed that God cares about even the minute details of our lives. What I learned was that even when you don't have much, you still have God.

When I was kidnapped by the Taliban, my life was no longer my own. The most basic choices that most of us take for granted were suddenly out of my hands. No options. No freedom. No future. Yet even though I'd lost virtually everything, I still had God. I still had his Spirit to guide and comfort me. He was what I needed most then and is still what I need most today.

I cannot imagine anything sweeter.

ACKNOWLEDGMENTS

LIFE IS SO OFTEN THE BEAUTIFUL RESULT OF PEOPLE, PLACES, and situations, all playing their parts to bring about deeper purpose and meaning. I am indebted to many who have molded me into who I am today.

To my father and mother—I couldn't have asked for a better upbringing. Your sacrifices and your service to God, family, and others taught me the valuable lesson of striving for a balanced life. I am eternally grateful to God for choosing you both to raise me.

My sister Deepa and her family—Life simply wouldn't have the same meaning without you. Ever since Mom's death, you have taken on many different roles for my sake and for that of our extended family. You are a rock that many depend on, including me. Steve and my two beautiful nieces are great icing on the cake.

My extended family—I am so grateful for your continued voice in my life. My uncles and aunties from both sides of the family— your love and care during many milestones in my life continue to be defining factors that propel me forward. A special shout-out goes to Uncle Roy and Uncle Thomas. You both mean a lot to me, and I am so grateful for your support and devotion.

My work colleagues—If it wasn't for the dedication and tireless effort from all of you—Daniel, Lars, John, Paul, Lori, Joan, Adrienne, Roy, Grace, Akram, Al, Ken, Debbie, and all of you in Afghanistan—I simply wouldn't be here today. I am so grateful that our paths have crossed. Thank you for demonstrating what is of greatest value on almost a daily basis.

My two colleagues who were in captivity with me, Rafiq and Farzad—I am deeply indebted to both of you. Your bravery and calm demeanor throughout our captivity helped me keep my composure during one of the most difficult experiences of my life. I don't know what I would have done without the two of you.

Matthew, David, and Sam—You deserve a special note here. Upon my return the last thing I wanted to do was talk about what I had gone through with the Taliban. I received sound advice not to expect people to understand what I had just experienced. But talking to you three made me realize that this is a story to be shared. Your listening ears and gentle spirits made it easy for me to open up. It also helped tremendously that you had traveled on the same road where I had been captured.

Duane and Sam—I *love* our monthly get-togethers. I love that I can talk about anything with you guys. The word *friendship* has more meaning because of the two of you.

Vidu—You have been the brother I never had. You have played a significant role in my life since high school. Thank you for still believing in me and supporting me in so many ways. I am still hoping that we don't have to live so far away from each other.

Jim—I still remember the first time I met you. I couldn't help but wonder how this process of being an "open book" to a complete stranger was actually going to work. In a matter of a few months, you became not only a close friend but also "Uncle Jim" to my kids. Many times when it seemed our deadline was going to be hard to meet, your incredible gift of putting my thoughts into words, along with your patient demeanor, has gotten us through. I have a book I'm extremely proud of mainly due to you, my friend.

Joel—Since you have decided to pull the curtain on this chapter of your life as a literary agent, here is one wish that this book will become one of your legacies. I want you to know that if it wasn't for your easygoing manner, I would not have signed up for this project. Also, your insight in bringing Jim into the picture was a classic example of your sheer genius. I wish you much success in the next chapter of your journey.

Debbie—I can't believe that I have yet to meet you because it feels like I have known you for years. Your belief and enthusiasm and gentle probing have moved this project along in record pace. I can't wait to meet you and celebrate! And, yes, I also have enjoyed your twenty e-mails each day over the past several months. We would not have made it without your oversight—well done. My sincerest gratitude goes out to you and the entire team at Thomas Nelson for all your tireless efforts.

Nic—There is now one more thing I have added to the list of what I will not understand on this side of heaven. To rescue me, you paid the ultimate sacrifice. While your legacy will live on in my life and that of my family, my prayer is that many who read this story will be inspired by the example of your intentional service to make their own choices to live sacrificially for their families, communities, and nation.

My new friends at the FBI, in the military, and in other sectors of government—Before this event, I didn't even know that the FBI had a citizen's service department. All of you have served me and my family so beautifully. Because of your care, I feel that I have made it through this event unharmed.

The people of Afghanistan—The world knows very little about you, and that little doesn't portray who you really are. My experience has revealed so much more. Your resolve, pride, resilience, and camaraderie bring a beauty that the world simply needs to know. My wish and prayer is that you stand up against what is bad and stand up for the truth that brings life. This world has much to learn from you.

Cilicia, Asha, Jaron, Tobi, Eshaan, and the baby—You bring me *life* every day. Not a single day is the same, and I love it. All of you love me for who I am and help make me who I want to be. I couldn't ask for more. I appreciate the role you play to enable me to equip others who are in greater need.

To you, the reader—I am grateful for your choice to read this book. It is my hope that you now see Afghanistan in a different and more comprehensive light. Perhaps you will even accept the challenge to personally experience this nation and its people. If so, you will never be the same—and I mean that in the best of ways.

—Dilip Joseph

DILIP JOSEPH IS A REMARKABLE MAN. THE SAME EASYGOING manner, positive attitude, and unshakable faith that served him so well during a kidnapping by the Taliban also enabled him to put up with months of my endless questions. Thank you, Dilip, for your patience and your friendship, for your heart for all people in this world, and for the window into the life of an amazing servant. You have taught me more than you know.

To Cilicia, Asha, Jaron, Tobi, and Eshaan. Thank you for welcoming me into your home and making me feel like part of the family. I can't wait to come back and read more bedtime stories.

Daniel, Lars, and everyone at Morning Star who was so helpful during my visit there. I admire you all for bringing much-needed peace and hope to the world.

Everyone who made my research trip to Afghanistan such an amazing experience. Lars, thanks for being my last-minute tour guide to Kabul—and for loaning your clothes when my luggage didn't show. Mahmoud and family in Dubai, I so appreciated your hospitality. So many others contributed in multiple ways, including Al, Aref, Bruce, Debbie, Faith, Gabriella, Jerry, John, Ken, Mary Beth, Ron, Sheila, Sofia, Stephanie, Theresa, and the native team members. You all have my best wishes and gratitude.

Special thanks to Farzad and, especially, Rafiq, who took the time to sit down and share some of the most difficult memories imaginable. My new brother, I so admire your courage and your commitment to the people of Afghanistan.

Joel Kneedler, I've enjoyed every minute of our work together and wish you and the family all the best in the years ahead. I need to figure out a way to get you back to central Oregon.

Debbie Wickwire and the team at Thomas Nelson, your enthusiasm and dedication continue to be a joy. Let's do many more of these.

My thanks to other contributors to this project, including Gary and Julie Williams, Angela Lund, Bob Green, David Lund, Paulmer Soderberg, and Debi Cummings.

Last but not least, my deepest appreciation for the continuing support of my family: Angela, Erik, Sonja, Peter, Dad, and Dave.

—James Lund

NOTES

CHAPTER 2: AFGHANISTAN

1. "Population (Total)," The World Bank, accessed July 8, 2014, http://data.worldbank.org/indicator/SP.POP.TOTL?page=1.
2. "Afghanistan Population 2013," World Population Statistics, accessed July 8, 2014, www.worldpopulationstatistics.com/afghanistan-population-2013/.
3. "Afghan authorities tackle country's high illiteracy rate," United Nations Missions Assistance in Afghanistan, September 8, 2013, http://unama.unmissions.org/Default.aspx?ctl=Details&tabid=12254&mid=15756&ItemID=37242.
4. "Afghan life expectancy has risen by 17 years since 2001," Progressive Economy, February 13, 2014, http://progressive-economy.org/2014/02/13/afghan-life-expectancy-has-risen-by-17-years-since-2001/.
5. "Mortality rate, under-5 (per 1,000 live births)," The World Bank, http://data.worldbank.org/indicator/SH.DYN.MORT?page=1.
6. "Afghanistan's poppy farmers plant record opium crop, UN report says," *The Guardian*, November 13, 2013, www.theguardian.com/world/2013/nov/13/afghanistan-record-opium-crop-poppies-un.

CHAPTER 3: ANGUISH AND PEACE

1. "Afghanistan's ethnic diversity," CNN.com/asia, August 19, 2009, www.cnn.com/2009/WORLD/asiapcf/08/17/afghanistan.ethnic.groups/index.html?iref=24hours.
2. Daniel 3:17–18.

CHAPTER 9: THE CONVERSATION

1. "The World Factbook," Central Intelligence Agency, accessed July 8, 2014, www.cia.gov/library/publications/the-world-factbook/fields /2122.html.
2. Steve Coll, "Looking for Mullah Omar," *The New Yorker*, January 23, 2012, http://www.newyorker.com/reporting/2012/01/23/120123fa _fact_coll.
3. Ahmed Rashid, *Taliban: Islam, Oil, and the New Great Game in Central Asia* (New Haven, CT: Yale University Press, 2000), 87.

CHAPTER 13: "PAPA'S IN TROUBLE"

1. Matthew 10:28–31.

CHAPTER 19: HOME

1. Isaiah 6:8.

GLOSSARY

burqa: a long, loose garment covering the whole body from head to
feet, worn in public by many Muslim women

chadri: veil

Dari: one of two official languages of Afghanistan

ferengi: foreigner

Hazara: Persian-speaking Shiites living in Afghanistan, with popula-
tions largely concentrated in the central part of the country

ISAF: International Security Assistance Force, a NATO-sponsored
military presence in Afghanistan made up of troops from the
United States and other nations

Jirga: tribal council

Kuchis: nomads who earn a living by herding and selling sheep, goats,
donkeys, and camels

madrassa: Islamic religious school

mujahideen: Muslim freedom fighters

mullah: local Muslim religious leader

naan: leavened, oven-baked flatbread popular in west, central, and south Asia

namaz: ritual Islamic worship or prayer

NGO: non-governmental organization

pakol: soft, round-topped men's hat, typically wool, worn by ethnic groups living in or near the Hindu Kush mountain range

pani: water

Pashto: language spoken by Pashtuns; one of two official languages of Afghanistan

Pashtun: most common ethnic group in Afghanistan

Pashtunwali: a tribal honor code that governs the Pashtun way of life

salwar kameez: traditional Afghan attire consisting of long, loose shirt with pajama-like pants

shamshoby: a short, green shrub common in eastern Afghanistan

surma: an ore sometimes ground into a black powder and applied around the eyes

Taliban: plural of *Talib*, or "student, seeker of knowledge"; fundamentalist Muslim movement

taqiyah: a short, round skullcap

tashakor: thank you

Urdu: official language of Pakistan

Zakah: in Islamic tradition, the practice of giving from what Allah has already provided to others in need

RECOMMENDED RESOURCES

SEE THE FOLLOWING LIST OF LINKS AND OTHER RESOURCES:

AFGHANISTAN

www.afghan-web.com

an overview of Afghanistan and its people and culture

THE TALIBAN

Ahmed Rashid, *Taliban: Islam, Oil, and the New Great Game
in Central Asia* (New Haven, CT: Yale University Press, 2000)

account of the origins and rise of the Taliban and their
impact on the region and the world

U.S. NAVY SEALS

Marcus Luttrell with Patrick Robinson, *Lone Survivor* (New
York: Little, Brown and Company, 2007)

describes 2005 U.S. Navy SEALs mission and Taliban
attack in Afghanistan

Mark Owen with Kevin Maurer, *No Easy Day* (New York:
Dutton, 2012)

account of the 2011 raid on Osama bin Laden
compound in Abbottobod, Pakistan

Eric Blehm, *Fearless* (Colorado Springs, CO: WaterBrook, 2012)
the life and death of U.S. SEAL Team Six operator Adam
Brown

U.S. VETERANS SUPPORT

www.udtseal.org
home page of nonprofit organization devoted to
assisting those who have served or are serving in naval
special warfare

www.woundedwarriorproject.org
home page of nonprofit organization committed to
honoring and supporting injured service members

COMMUNITY DEVELOPMENT

www.chalmers.org
website of nonprofit community development
organization dedicated to helping the church alleviate
poverty

ABOUT THE AUTHORS

DILIP JOSEPH, MPH, MD, SERVES AS MEDICAL DIRECTOR OF Morning Star Development (MSDEV). He oversees the public health, preventive health, and clinical projects operated by MSDEV through its rural medical clinics in Afghanistan. He is responsible for training the medical staff, evaluating and improving the medical services, and expanding medical efforts through networking and fund-raising so MSDEV can cater to many more Afghans who do not have access to health care.

Dr. Joseph completed his undergraduate degree in biochemistry at Azusa Pacific University, his graduate degree in international public health at Loma Linda University, and his medical degree in England. His medical work spans both developing and developed countries with internships and work experiences in public health and clinical medicine. His interest lies in incorporating his medical experiences for the betterment of rural communities in the developing world.

Dr. Joseph has a passion to develop communities that would invest in a holistic perspective on health: physical wholeness as a result of a healthy interaction between body, soul, and spirit. It is his desire to see a shift in the conventional paradigm of physical wellness to one that is a natural result of a healthy physical, social, mental, and spiritual interaction.

JAMES LUND IS AN AWARD-WINNING COLLABORATOR AND EDI-tor and the coauthor of *A Dangerous Faith* and *Danger Calling*. He works with best-selling authors and public figures such as George Foreman, Kathy Ireland, Max Lucado, Tim Brown, Randy Alcorn, and Jim Daly. He lives with his family in Oregon. Visit his website at jameslundbooks.com.

Printed in the USA
CPSIA information can be obtained
at www.ICGtesting.com
LVHW051536210724
785408LV00010B/160